ONE 1 DAY

CHRISTMAS
— CRAFTS —

Publications International, Ltd.

Products used in *One-Day Christmas Crafts*:
(Available in most arts and crafts stores.)

Creamcoat by Delta Artist's Acrylic Paints
(Ho-Ho-Ho Santa Post, Well-Lit Welcome)

Black & Decker Two-Temperature Glue Gun
(Ho-Ho-Ho Santa Post)

DMC Embroidery Floss
(Dazzling Stitched Accessories, Christmas Cheer Mugs)

Kreinik Blager Heavy Braid
(Dazzling Stitched Accessories, Lacy Angel Vest)

Velcro Hook and Loop Tape
(Dazzling Stitched Accessories)

Maxwell International
black fabric cord
(Dazzling Stitched Accessories)

Fond Memories
acyrlic coasters
(Yuletide Coasters)

Daniel Enterprises
red mugs
(Christmas Cheer Mugs)

Liquitex Concentrated Artists Colors
Yellow Light and Laquer Red
(Poinsettia Place Settings)

Deka Permanent Fabric Paint
Medium Green
(Poinsettia Place Settings)

DecoArt Fabric Acrylic Paints
Heavy Metals Light (Diamond Yellow, Sparkling Ruby),
Shimmering Pearls (Lime Green)
(Poinsettia Place Settings)

Tulip Paint Writer (Yellow)
(Poinsettia Place Settings)
Colorpoint and Glitter Fabric Paint
(Dancing Gingerbread Tree Skirt)

Majestic Bendable Ribbon
(Poinsettia Place Settings)

Sculpey Colored Modeling Compound
(Family Fun Project)

Therm O Web, Inc.
HeatnBond Originial No-Sew adhesive
(Lacy Angel Vest, Satin Wreath Sweatshirt, Dancing
Gingerbread Tree Skirt)

Marvy Fabric Marker
(Lacy Angel Vest)

THE BEADERY Craft Products
Rhinestones, faceted stones, stars, cabochons, pony beads
(Lacy Angel Vest, Splendid Snowman Stocking)

Aleene's OK To Wash-It Fabric Glue
(Lacy Angel Vest)

Jones Tones Aurora Flakes and Aurora Dust Dimensional
Glitter; Stretch Fabric Paint: Enamels—Green, Red, Black;
Liquid Foil Pearl; Glitter Copper
(Peek-A-Boo T-Shirt, Dancing Gingerbread Tree Skirt)

Craft Designers: Beth Franks (pages 18, 21, 24, 56), Bev
George (pages 40, 54, 62), Joan Green (pages 15, 46, 48,
59), Kathy Lamancusa (pages 28, 34, 43, 50, 52), Delores
Ruzicka (pages 36, 38), The Beadery (page 31).

Contributing Writers: Betty Valle, Delores Ruzicka

Technical Advisor: Melissa Birdsong

Photography: Sacco Productions Limited/Chicago

Photographers: Tom O'Connell, Peter Ross

Photo Stylist: Diane Pronites

Models: Karen Blaschek, Sherrie Withers, Ashley
Pincus/Royal Model Management

CONTENTS

INTRODUCTION

Christmastide is the happiest time of the year for many people—children and adults alike! But time always seems at a premium—especially during the holidays. This is also the time when creating decorations and presents is most fun and fulfilling—and appreciated by those receiving lovingly made handcrafted gifts. With One-Day Christmas Crafts you have many exciting crafts that take less than a day to create. Things made by hand come from the heart.

The projects in this book include a wide variety of techniques and methods. Take a moment and look through the pages. You'll find everything from traditional counted cross-stitch to appliqué. Crafting at Christmas is a wonderful way to escape the crowded shopping malls and the mad race to find that "perfect" gift. Now you'll be able to make something wonderful for just about everyone on your gift list right at home—and they can all be made in less than a day! Each project has complete step-by-step instructions and photos to help make everything easy to understand and fun to do.

We hope you enjoy creating these projects. They are for all skill levels and interests, and you'll find that many of the projects use basic items you already have around your home. Once you begin, you'll see that creating your own gifts and holiday decorations is a satisfying and relaxing way to get ready for the holidays.

WHAT YOU'LL FIND

JEWELRY MAKING

Although the jewelry in this book looks sophisticated, most is made by gluing. Jewelry findings is a term for a variety of ready-made metal components used as attachments and fastenings to assemble jewelry. They are usually made of inexpensive metal. Findings include pin backs, earring findings, barrel clasps, jump rings, and beading wire—for our projects you will need a pin back and earring findings. All of these items are easily found in your local craft or hobby store.

POLYMER CLAY

There are several polymer clays on the market. All are intermixable and offer you endless options for creating different objects. The clays are quite hard when first unwrapped and must be kneaded until soft and pliable. Make sure not to use the clay before it reaches this stage—if you do, you may create air pockets and cracks when you roll it out. This can cause the clay to break apart. After you have worked your clay until it is soft, roll it into logs. You can proceed with your project at this point.

When you have finished forming your clay object, you will need to bake it to harden it. Follow instructions on package for baking times and temperatures— baking at the right time and temperature may take some practice. If you don't bake the clay long enough, it becomes crumbly, but if you bake it too long

you can burn it. When the clay comes out of the oven, it will be a bit soft; it hardens as it cools. It is best to bake the clay objects on a nonconducting surface, such as a thick, tempered glass (Pyrex®); slate; or ceramic pan.

Caution: Do not bake above 265 degrees Fahrenheit, and use a separate thermometer to verify actual oven temperature. Do not overbake, as fumes could be toxic. If you lengthen the baking time, lower the temperature to 250 degrees Fahrenheit. Do not swallow polymer clay, and supervise children at all times when baking.

CROSS-STITCH

Cross-stitch is traditionally worked on an "even-weave" cloth that has vertical and horizontal threads of equal thickness and spacing. Six-strand embroidery floss is used for most stitching; there are also many beautiful threads that can be used to enhance the appearance of the stitching. Finishing and framing a counted cross-stitch piece will complete your work. There are many options in framing—just visit your local craft shop or framing gallery.

Basic Supplies

Fabric: The most common even-weave fabric is 14-count Aida cloth. The weave of this fabric creates distinct squares that make stitching very easy for the beginner.

Needles, Hoops, and Scissors: A blunt-end or tapestry needle is used for counted cross-stitch. A #24 needle is the recommended size for stitching on 14-count Aida cloth. You may use an embroidery hoop while stitching—just be sure to remove it when not working on your project. A small pair of sharp scissors are a definite help when working with embroidery floss.

Floss: Six-strand cotton embroidery floss is most commonly used, and it's usually cut into 18-inch lengths for stitching. Use two of the six strands for stitching on 14-count Aida cloth. Also use two strands for backstitching.

Preparing to Stitch

The materials list will tell you what size piece of cloth to use. To locate the center of the design, lightly fold your fabric in half and in half again. Find the center of the chart by following the arrows on the sides.

Reading the chart is easy, since each square on the chart equals one stitch on the fabric. The colors correspond to the floss numbers listed in the color key. Select a color and stitch all of that color within an area. Begin by holding the thread ends behind the fabric until secured or covered over with two or three stitches. You may skip a few stitches on the back of the material, but do not run the thread from one area to another behind a section that will not be stitched in the finished piece—it will show through the fabric. If your thread begins to twist, drop the needle and allow the thread to untwist. It is important to the final appearance of the project to keep an even tension when pulling stitches through so that all stitches will have a uniform look. To end a thread, weave or run the thread under several stitches on the back side. Cut the ends close to the fabric.

Each counted cross-stitch is represented by a colored square on the project's chart. For horizontal rows, work the stitches in two steps, i.e., all of the left to right stitches and then all of the right to left stitches (see Figure A). For vertical rows, work each complete stitch as shown in Figure B. Three-quarter stitches are often used when the design requires two colors in one square or to allow more detail in the pattern (See Figure C). The backstitch is often used to outline or create letters, and is shown by bold lines on the patterns. Backstitch is usually worked after the pattern is completed (See Figure D).

Fig. A
Cross-stitch

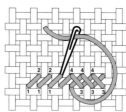

Fig. B
Vertical Cross-stitch

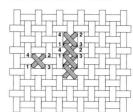

Fig. C
Three-quarter Stitches

Fig. D
Backstitching

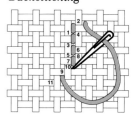

PLASTIC CANVAS

Plastic canvas allows for three-dimensional stitchery projects to be constructed. Stitching on plastic canvas is easy to do, easy on the eyes, and easy on the pocketbook, too.

Basic Supplies

Plastic Canvas: Canvas is most widely available by the sheet. Stitch all the pieces of a project on the same brand of plastic canvas to ensure that the meshes will match when you join them together.

Plastic canvas comes in several counts or mesh sizes (number of stitches to the inch) and numerous sizes of sheets. Specialty sizes and shapes such as circles are also available. Most canvas is clear, although up to 24 colors are available. Colored canvas is used when parts of the project remain unstitched. Seven-count canvas comes in four weights—standard; a thinner flexible weight; a stiffer, rigid weight; and a softer weight made especially for bending and curved projects. Designs can be stitched on any mesh count—the resulting size of the project is the only thing that will be affected. The smaller the count number, the larger the project will be, since the count number refers to the number of stitches per inch. Therefore, seven-count has seven stitches per inch, while 14-count has 14. A 14-

The following stitches are used in plastic canvas:

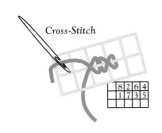

Work the plastic canvas **cross-stitch** just as you do a regular cross-stitch.

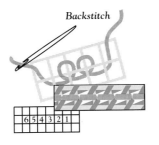

Work the plastic canvas **back-stitch** just as you do a cross-stich backstitch.

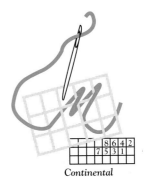

For the **continental stitch,** your needle comes up at 1 and all odd-numbered holes and goes down at 2 and all even-numbered holes.

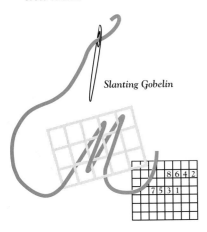

For the **slanting gobelin stitch,** your needle comes up at 1 and all odd-numbered holes and goes down at 2 and all even-numbered holes. Follow pattern.

For the **French knot,** bring your needle up at one hole and wrap yarn clockwise around needle. Holding the yarn, insert needle in the hole to the right and slowly pull yarn.

For the **overcast stitch,** the needle goes down at the numbered holes, and the yarn wraps over the edge of the canvas. Make sure to cover the canvas completely.

count project will be half the size of a 7-count project if two identical projects were stitched on 7-count and 14-count canvas.

Needles: Needle size is determined by the count size of the plastic canvas you are using. Patterns generally call for a #18 needle for stitching on 7-count plastic canvas, a #16 or #18 for 10-count canvas, and a #22 or #24 for stitching on 14-count plastic canvas.

Yarns: A wide variety of yarns may be used. The most common is worsted weight (or 4-ply). Acrylic yarns are less expensive and washable; wool may also be used. Several companies produce specialty yarns for plastic canvas work. These cover the canvas well and will not "pill" as some acrylics do. Sport weight yarn (or 3-ply) and embroidery floss are often used on 10-count canvas. Use 12 strands or double the floss thickness for 10-count canvas and 6 strands for stitching on 14-count canvas. On 14-count plastic canvas, many of the specialty metallic threads made for cross-stitch can be used to highlight and enhance your project.

Cutting Out Your Project

Many plastic canvas projects are dimensional—a shape has to be cut out and stitched. Scissors or a craft knife are recommended.

Preparing to Stitch

Cut your yarn to a 36-inch length. Begin by holding the yarn end behind the fabric until secured or covered over with two or three stitches. To end a length, weave or run the yarn under several stitches on the back side. Cut the end close to the canvas. The continental stitch is the most commonly used stitch to cover plastic canvas. Decorative stitches will add interest and texture to your project. As in cross-stitch, if your yarn begins to twist, drop the needle and allow the yarn to untwist. It is important to the final appearance of the project to keep an even tension when pulling your stitches through so that all of your stitch-es have a uniform look. Do not pull your stitches too tight, since this causes gaps in your stitching and allows the canvas to show through between your stitches. Also, do not carry one color yarn across too many rows of another color on the back—the carried color may show through to the front of your project. Do not stitch the outer edge of the canvas until the other stitching is complete. If the project is a single piece of canvas, overcast the outer edge with the color specified. If there are two or more pieces, follow the pattern instructions for assembly.

Cleaning

If projects are stitched with acrylic yarn, they may be washed by hand using warm or cool water and a mild detergent. Place on a terry cloth towel to air dry. Do not place in a dryer or dry clean.

WEARABLES

You'll find fabric painting to be fast, easy, and fun. With the latest development in fabric paints, using basic dimensional paints is almost as easy as writing with a ballpoint pen. Some of the painting projects will require a brush—we'll tell you what type of brush you'll need in the project's materials list.

Using a Shirt Board

You might want a commercially purchased shirt board, or you can make your own by cutting corrugated cardboard into the shape of a flattened T-shirt about 1/2 inch smaller than the shirt you'll be using. Cover it with wax paper and insert it into the item you'll be working on—it will prevent paint from bleeding through, and it will make it easier for you to transport a project with wet paint. Make sure the waxed side is under the surface you want to paint.

Paints: Each of the projects will specify the type of paints required. Only dimensional and embellished paints, which are especially formulated to use on fabric, are used. For specific instructions for each paint, follow the instructions on the packaging or bottle.

Basic Guidelines for Wearables

1. Prewash fabric and sweatshirt without using any softeners. Softeners prevent the paint from bonding completely with the fibers. Press out any wrinkles.

2. If you're right-handed, work on your project from the upper left-hand corner to the lower right-hand corner. Paint all colors

as you go. This will prevent you from accidentally smearing the paint with your elbow or hand.

3. When using dimensional paints, pick up the tube of paint with the cap on and shake the paint down into the tip to remove any air bubbles each time you use a color. Place a paint bottle down on its side between uses.

4. Hold your dimensional paint bottle like a ballpoint pen. Squeeze gently to push out paint. Work quickly and smoothly. Moving too slowly often results in a "bumpy" appearance.

5. When using dimensional glitter paint, be sure to draw a line of paint that is thick enough to carry the glitter.

6. Allow paints to dry at least 6 to 8 hours before touching. Allow 36 to 48 hours for paint to be completely cured before wearing.

Caring For Your Wearable

Hand or machine wash in lukewarm water—NOT COLD!!—in delicate/knit cycle. Cold water will crack the paint. Tumble dry on low for a few minutes to remove wrinkles, then remove and lay flat to dry. Do not wash in Woolite or other delicate care wash products.

Sewing

The excitement of making your own holiday crafts sometimes gets in the way of your preparation. Before plunging into your chosen project, check to make sure you have all the materials needed. Being prepared will make your sewing easier and more fun. Most of the items you need will probably be on hand already.

Scissors: Two styles are needed, one about eight to ten inches long with bent handles for cutting fabric. This style of scissors allows you to cut through the fabric while the fabric lays flat. These shears should be sharp and used only for fabric. The second style of scissors is smaller, about six inches, with sharp points. You will need this style for smaller projects and close areas.

Straight Pins: Nonrusting dressmaker pins are best. They will not leave rust marks on your fabric if they come in contact with dampness or glue. And dressmaker's pins have very sharp points for easy insertion.

Tape Measure: Should be plastic coated so that it will not stretch and could be wiped off if it comes in contact with paint or glue.

Ironing Board and Steam Iron: Be sure your ironing board is well padded and has a clean covering. Sometimes you do more sewing with the iron than you do with the sewing machine. Keeping your fabrics, seams, and hems pressed cuts down on stitches and valuable time. A steam or dry iron is best. It is important to press your fabric to achieve a professional look. The iron is also used to adhere the fusible adhesive. Keep the bottom of your iron clean and free of any substance that could mark your fabric. The steam iron may be used directly on most fabrics with no shine. Test a small piece of the fabric first. If it causes a shine on the right side, try the reverse side.

Thread: Have mercerized sewing thread in the colors needed for each project you have chosen. Proper shade and strength (about a 50 weight) of thread avoids having the stitching show more than is necessary and the item will have a finished look.

Fusible Adhesive: Fusible adhesive is placed paper side up on wrong side of material. Place iron on paper side of adhesive and press for one to three seconds. Allow fabric to cool. Design can then be drawn or traced onto the paper side and cut out. Remove the paper and place the material right side up in desired position on project and iron for three to five seconds.

Sewing Machine: Neat, even stitches are achieved in a very few minutes with a sewing-machine. If desired, you may machine-stitch a zigzag stitch around the attached fusible adhesive pieces to secure the edges.

Work Surface: Your sewing surface should be a comfortable height for sitting and roomy enough to lay out your projects. Keep it clean and free of other crafting materials that could accidentally spill or soil your fabric.

THE BAND SAW

The band saw is a very handy, easy-to-use tool for the home workshop. It may be easily operated by a man, woman, or an older child with supervision. A band saw may sit on your workbench or it may also have its own legs or stand. Band saws do not take up much space.

Respect your band saw—Safety First! Before you begin to saw, read your instruction manual. Always keep in mind these simple safety hints:

Keep your work area clean and uncluttered.
Don't use band saw in damp or wet locations.
Keep your work area well lit.
Do not force band saw to saw through items that it is not designed for.
Wear proper clothing—nothing loose or baggy.
Wear safety goggles.
Never leave band saw running unattended.

One advantage of the band saw is its versatility. The fast-cutting saw uses a flexible steel blade, in the form of a continuous loop, that runs over two rubber wheels. To use the saw, feed the wood into the blade. For straight, fast cutting, use a wide, coarse-toothed blade; for curve cutting, use a narrower blade. Don't try to turn corners that are too tight for the blade width; if you do, the blade will burn and the wood may become wedged onto the saw blade. The $3/_{26}$-inch blade will cut a 1-inch circle, the $1/_2$-inch blade will cut a $2^1/_2$-inch circle, and the $3/_4$-inch blade will cut a $3^1/_2$-inch circle.

When operating the saw, set the upper blade guide about $1/_4$ to $1/_2$ inch above the work. Band saw blades are reasonably priced and stay sharp a long time. It is practical to throw away the old ones rather than to sharpen them. Never use a dull blade!

Most band saws are equipped with a tilting table for beveling and for cutting objects at an angle. Sometimes it is necessary to turn the work upside down to make certain parts of a cut. After practicing with your band saw, you will become more comfortable with it.

A WORD ABOUT GLUE

Glue can be a sticky subject when you don't use the right one for the job. There are many different glues on the craft market today, each formulated for a different crafting purpose.

The following are ones you should be familiar with:

White Glue: This may be used as an all-purpose glue—when dry it is clear and flexible. It is often referred to as craft glue or tacky glue. Tacky on contact, it allows you to put two items together without a lot of set up time required. Use for most projects, especially ones involving wood, plastics, some fabrics, and cardboard.

Thin-Bodied Glues: Use these glues when your project requires a smooth, thin layer of glue. Thin-bodied glues work well on some fabrics and papers.

Fabric Glue: This type of glue is made to bond with fabric fibers and withstand repeated washing. Use this kind of glue for attaching rhinestones and/or other charms to fabric projects. Some glues require heat-setting. Check the bottle for complete instructions.

Hot Melt Glue: Formed into cylindrical sticks, this glue is inserted into a hot temperature glue gun and heated to liquid state. Depending on the type of glue gun used, the glue is forced out through the gun's nozzle by either pushing on the end of the glue stick or squeezing a trigger. Use clear glue sticks for projects using wood, fabrics, most plastics, ceramics, and cardboard. When using any glue gun, be careful of the nozzle and the freshly applied glue—it is very hot! Apply glue to the piece being attached. Work with small areas at a time so that the glue doesn't set before being pressed into place.

Low Melt Glue: This is similar to hot melt glues in that it is formed into sticks and requires a glue gun to be used. Low melt glues are used for projects that would be damaged by heat. Examples include foam, balloons, and metallic ribbons. Low melt glue sticks are oval-shaped and can only be used in a low-temperature glue gun.

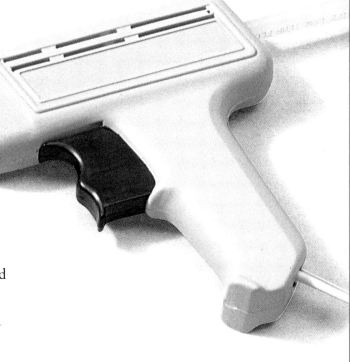

HAPPY HOLIDAY HAIR BOWS

Bows add the crowning

glory to holiday attire.

Whether ruffled with

pearls and beads or looped

with bells, add a festive

touch to your wardrobe.

Materials

Looped Barrette:

3¾-inch barrette

Spool wire

Wire cutters

1⅜ yards ribbon, 1½ inches wide

1 yard gathered ribbon

6 small jingle bells

Fabric glue

Ruffled Ribbon:

1 yard ribbon, 2½ inches wide

Needle and thread

44 pearl beads

20 plated beads

2¾-inch barrette

1 For looped barrette: Open barrette and remove spring by pinching and pulling at center. Set spring aside. Slip wire through hole in end of barrette and twist to secure. Wrap wire around barrette several times.

2 Pinch ribbon about three inches from wired end. Place on barrette at wired end and wrap wire around ribbon and barrette several times to secure.

3 Pull up about 3 inches of ribbon and make a loop about 1½ inches tall. Pinch ribbon and wrap wire around ribbon and barrette several times to secure. Continue making loops and securing them to barrette with wire. You should be able to make approximately 12 loops and still have a 3-inch tail of ribbon at end of barrette.

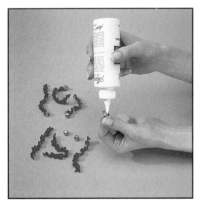

4 Slip wire through hole at end of barrette and twist to secure. Trim wire end. Trim ribbon ends at an angle. Replace spring in barrette. Cut gathered ribbon into lengths, two each of 4½ inches, 4 inches, and 3½ inches. Glue bells at one end of ribbons and glue other ends between loops.

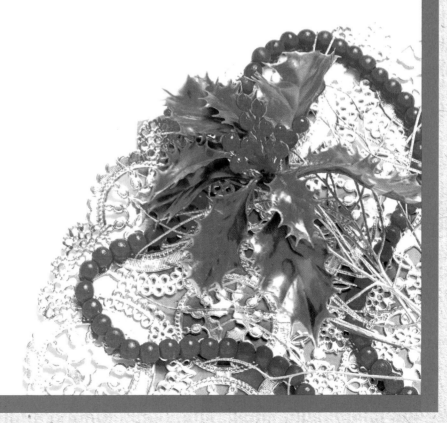

1 For ruffled ribbon: Fold ribbon in half lengthwise and make a faint crease; follow crease as you sew. Secure thread at one end of ribbon in the center using a double stitch. The thread should be doubled and knotted at end. Sew a running stitch down crease. Stitches should be approximately ½ inch apart.

2 Hold ribbon in one hand and thread ends in other. Carefully pull thread in one direction and push ribbon in the other to create ruffle. When ruffle is desired length, tie or sew thread ends securely. Trim thread.

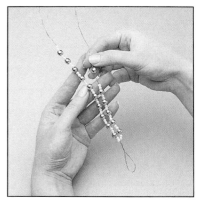

3 Cut off 16 inches of wire. Bend spool wire in half and twist a few times at end with the bend. Thread half the beads on one side of wire and half the beads on the other side in an alternating pattern—two pearl beads followed by one plated bead.

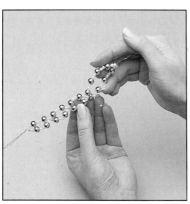

4 Twist wire at every other group of pearl beads to create a pattern as shown. Do not twist last group at either end of wire.

5 Place beaded wire lengthwise across top of ruffle. Bring ends of wire around back of ruffle and twist them together securely. Trim any excess wire.

6 Glue barrette to back of ruffle.

LACY ANGEL VEST

A vest magically becomes a holiday—frosted with lace trim and a winsome angel, accented with sparkling jewels. All this was made with an iron and some paint!

Materials

1 yard fusible adhesive

½ yard scalloped border lace, with star motif

Iron

Wax paper

Man's vest

12 × 6 inches white washable satin

Brown fabric marker

Muslin scraps (3 × 6 inches)

15m ombre metallic thread

Fabric paint: ivory, gold glitter

20 crystal acrylic rhinestones, 7mm and 8mm

Fabric glue

1 Lay back side of lace on fusible adhesive and cover with wax paper. Place iron on medium setting on wax paper and press for three to five seconds, flip over and iron on paper side of adhesive and press for another three seconds. Pull wax paper off lace while still warm. Let cool. Pull lace off paper and cut into desired shapes (extra adhesive will stick to lace in sheet form, trim when cutting shapes; adhesive in the holes will melt into fabric). Leave four stars uncut for angel wings.

2 Iron adhesive to back of satin and muslin. Place iron on medium setting on paper side of adhesive, press for three to five seconds. Trace patterns on the paper back of prepared materials. Use white for two angel dresses and muslin for two head circles. Cut out and peel paper off appliqués.

3 Place scalloped border around neckline of vest and top of left pocket. Assemble angels, one on right side of vest and one on back. Position extra lace stars around vest. Iron to adhere pieces.

4 With marker, draw face on head following pattern. Make 14 loopy pom-pons by winding metallic thread around two fingers 12 times; tie off in center using a separate piece of thread. Glue seven pom-pons around each angel's head using fabric glue.

5 Outline lace and stars with gold fabric paint and angel with ivory fabric paint (rest tip on edge to steady line). Add ivory dots to make extra fill-in stars. Glue rhinestones to vest with fabric glue.

DAZZLING STITCHED ACCESSORIES

A plastic canvas belt, brooch, and earrings add sparkle to even the plainest outfit. Make a striking fashion statement!

Materials

Belt:

- 1/3 sheet clear plastic canvas, #10 mesh
- Tapestry needles, #20 and #24
- 4 skeins black embroidery floss
- Metallic thread, 1 spool each red, green, gold
- 49 gold beads, 3mm each
- 1 1/2-inches hook and loop tape, 5/8 inch wide
- Black sewing thread and needle
- 6mm presewn black fabric cord, double waist size plus 6 inches

Belt Instructions:

Cut plastic canvas 69 holes × 36 holes. Trim according to pattern lines. Use small manicure scissors or craft knife to trim shaded areas for slots for cording.

Stitching: Using #20 needle, work metallic portions of design in continental stitch. Fill in background in continental stitch using black floss. To stitch with floss, cut a 2-yard length of floss, double it (making 12 strands), and thread cut ends through needle. Bring needle through canvas, holding looped end on back side. Make first stitch and pass needle through loop on back. Draw thread firmly to secure floss to canvas. When finished stitching, overcast outer edge and inside slots using double strand of black.

Attach beads to belt using a double strand of sewing thread and #24 needle. Knot end of thread and weave into stitching on back. Bring needle to front at point marked on chart for bead placement, slip a bead on needle and insert needle back through the same hole. When all beads are attached, knot end of thread and weave in ends securely.

Cut fabric cord in half. Fold one piece of cord in half and attach to side of belt with lark's head knot (see picture below) through slot. Place belt around waist and pin hook and loop tape strips. Pull fabric cord covering back ¾ inch and remove a small amount of core material. Turn fabric ends in and sew strips in place, sewing through all layers to secure.

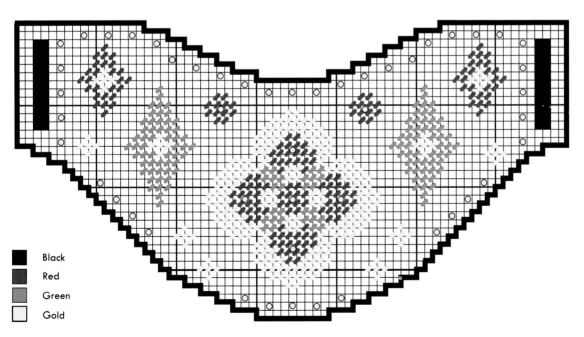

- ■ Black
- ▨ Red
- ▨ Green
- □ Gold

Materials

Brooch and Earrings:

⅙ sheet plastic canvas, #10 mesh

Metallic thread, 5 yards gold, 3 yards green, 2 yards red

15 gold beads, 3mm each

1 bar pin

1 set pierced earring findings (post-type)

Glue gun

Brooch and Earrings Instructions:
Cut one piece canvas 23 holes × 23 holes and two pieces 11 holes × 15 holes. Trim according to pattern lines. Stitch brooch and earrings entirely in continental stitch. Overcast all edges with gold. Attach beads according to belt instructions.

Use glue gun to attach bar pin to back of brooch. Glue earring posts to back of earrings.

PEEK·A·BOO T·SHIRT

Just a few snips reveal the bright green fabric peek-a-boo tree! Add red paint and glitter for sparkling pizzazz.

Materials

T-shirt

12-inch-square green Christmas material

Straight pins

Sewing machine

White thread

Pinking shears

Fabric paint: green, red

Fabric glitter

Craft knife

60 heart pony beads, assortment of solid and translucent red, two shades of green

Scissors

1 Copy and enlarge pattern. Turn T-shirt inside out (sewing is done on inside). Place Christmas fabric (right side down) centered, 1 inch from neck ribbing. Position paper tree pattern on top of material, and pin three layers (single layer of T-shirt, Christmas material, paper pattern) together. Use a lot of pins so fabrics won't shift and pleat.

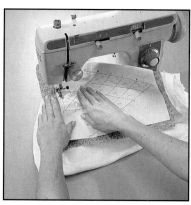

2 Machine stitch on top of pattern lines starting in bottom left corner: A (stitch to)> M > L > B > C > K > J > D > E > I > H > F > G. Now change angle but DON'T CUT THREAD, at bottom right corner G > M > N > F > E > O > P > D > C > Q > R > B > A. At bottom left corner, DON'T CUT THREAD, A > S > V > U > T > V > U > S > G. Cut thread.

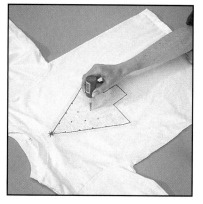

3 Remove paper (paper is perforated due to stitch line); it will rip away. Trim excess Christmas fabric with pinking shears, within $1/2$ inch of outside tree seam. Reverse shirt. Outline tree and trunk with fine line of green fabric paint. For ornaments, add small red dots at stitching intersections. Sprinkle wet paint with fabric glitter. Let dry. Shake off excess glitter. Don't wash shirt for 72 hours.

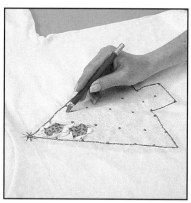

4 Using craft knife, make a small slit in center of stitched diamond (top layer only). Cut from center to each point, then cut each quarter flap in half again. This will give eight points to diamonds.

5 Fold up bottom of shirt four inches, with right sides together, and pin. Mark cutting lines about $2^1/2$ to 3 inches long and $1/4$ inch apart around shirt.

6 Cut on marked lines, through both layers of T-shirt. Cut three strips across fold, then skip one. Repeat around shirt. Remove pins.

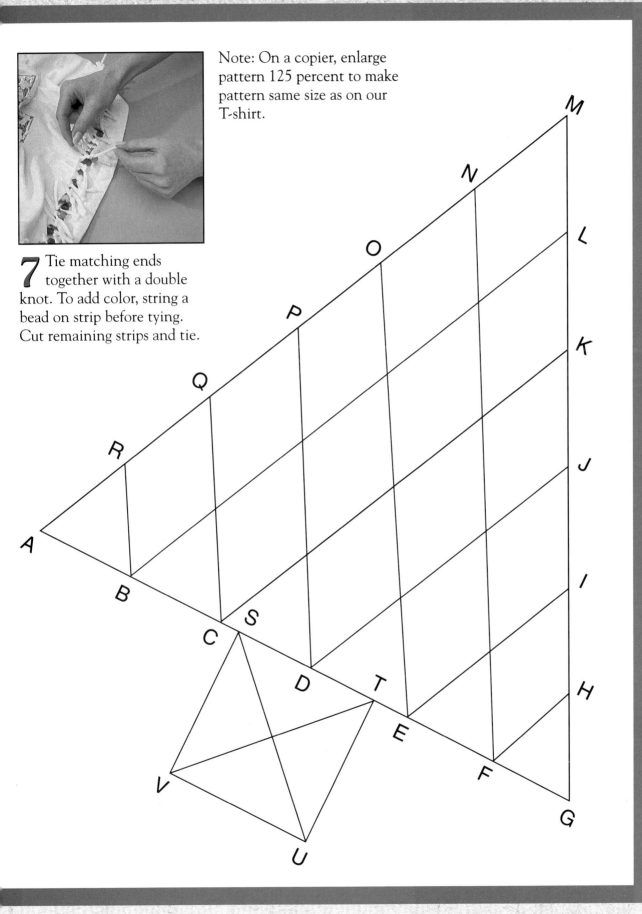

Note: On a copier, enlarge pattern 125 percent to make pattern same size as on our T-shirt.

7 Tie matching ends together with a double knot. To add color, string a bead on strip before tying. Cut remaining strips and tie.

SATIN WREATH SWEATSHIRT

Who would have thought that a black sweatshirt could be so elegant—and so easy to make! With an iron and some paint, you can create your favorite and most comfortable holiday attire.

Materials

Black sweatshirt

Iron

Freezer paper

⅓ yard washable green satin

⅓ yard washable red satin

1 yard fusible adhesive

Fabric paint: red, green, gold glitter

1 Reverse sweatshirt. Iron wax side of freezer paper to inside of sweatshirt neckline (front and back). Turn sweatshirt right side out.

4 Rest tip of fabric paint bottle on appliqué/ sweatshirt edge and outline leaves with green, berries with red, and bow with gold. All neckline pieces must be connected with paint to lock the sweatshirt when cut. If there are large empty spaces at neckline, small dots of gold can be added for filler and color. Add detail lines to center of holly and to bow (follow finished picture). Let dry 24 hours.

2 Iron fusible adhesive to back of red and green satin. Place iron on medium setting and iron paper side of adhesive, press for three to five seconds. Trace patterns on the paper back of prepared satin. Use red for bow, bow knot, and bow ties, and five to eight berries. Use green for 13 to 16 small and 5 to 7 large holly leaves. Cut out and peel paper off appliqué pieces.

5 Cut neckline ribbing away, following the appliqué wreath. Cut line should be as close to paint line as possible, without cutting paint.

3 Place bow off-center, about 1/2 inch from neckline. Place bow ties below bow. Place holly leaves and berries around neckline, filling in spaces as you go. Design will vary depending on size of sweatshirt. Cut one or two holly leaves from scraps to fill in holes (such as above knot on bow). Iron pieces as you are happy with the placement; be sure all edges are secured. Reiron if necessary, but do not overheat (iron three to seven seconds only).

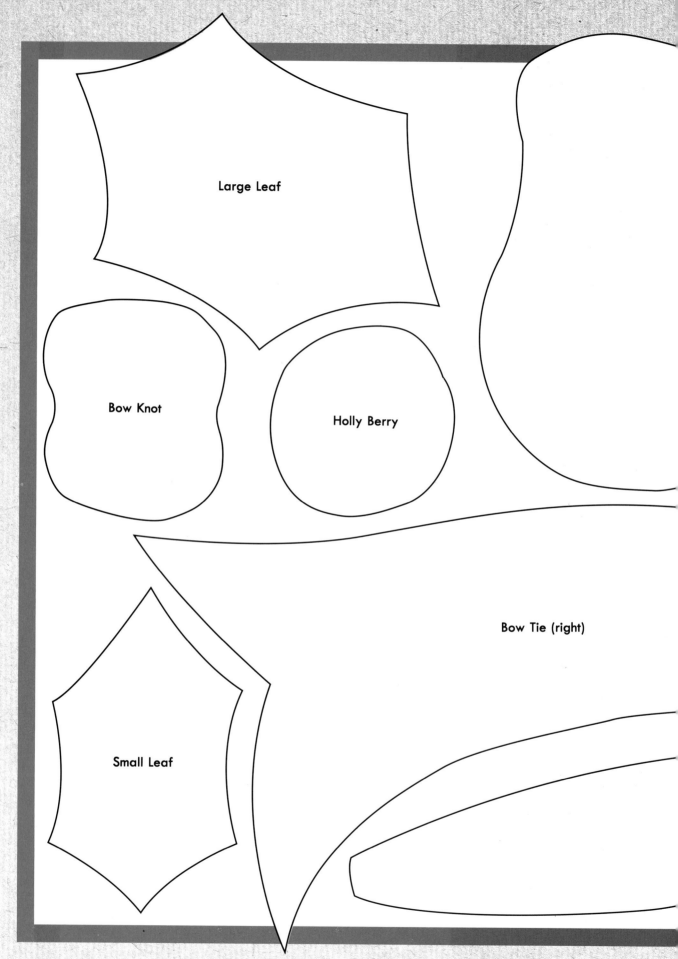

Large Leaf

Bow Knot

Holly Berry

Bow Tie (right)

Small Leaf

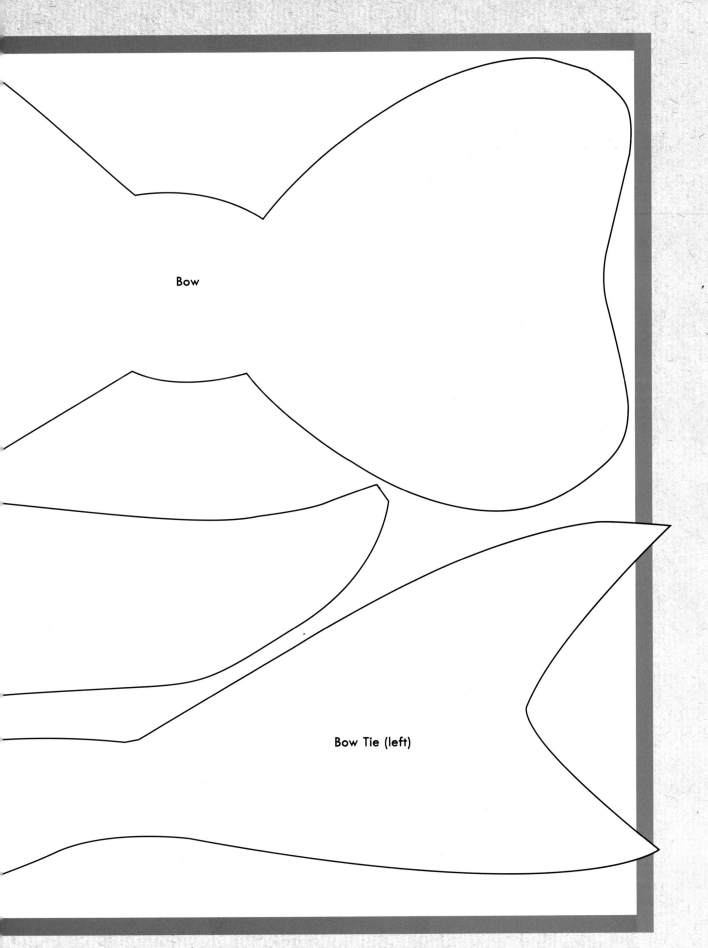

Bow

Bow Tie (left)

FRENCH HORN WALL HANGING

The blending of French horn, pine boughs, ribbons, and flowers will create musical memories!

Materials

1 block dried floral foam

1-ounce package green moss

Craft pins

14-inch brass French horn

6 silver tinseled pine stems, 16 inches each

Wire cutters

6 green pine sprays, 16 inches each

3 yards red plaid ribbon, 2⅝ inches wide

Wired wood picks

3 yards metallic gold musical note ribbon, 1¼ inches wide

5 gold poinsettias, 3 inches each

2 holly berry sprays, 8 inches each

Chenille stem

Tacky glue

1 Cover foam block with moss and pin in place with craft pins.

2 Secure French horn to top edge of foam block with craft pins. You can also wire horn in place.

3 Cut stems of two tinseled pine stems to a length of 12 inches. Insert one into each narrow end of floral foam. The pine should be placed under the horn.

4 Cut green pine sprays into seven-inch pieces. Randomly insert these around foam, forming the outside shape of the wallpiece. Pine should outline shape of horn.

5 Cut a two-yard length of the plaid ribbon and form a four-loop bow with two five-inch loops, two seven-inch loops, and two six-inch streamers. Using wired pick, attach bow to pick and insert into center of design.

6 Cut four lengths of gold ribbon, each 24 inches long. Form four-loop bows with three-inch streamers and no center loop. Attach each to a wooden pick and insert into design around plaid bow. Fill in around bow loops with remaining tinseled pine stems.

7 Cut two 12-inch streamers from gold ribbon and a 12-inch streamer from plaid ribbon. Secure each to a wooden pick. Insert plaid streamer below plaid bow (on side of horn bell). Insert gold streamers to left of plaid streamer.

8 Cut the stems of the poinsettias to a length of six inches. Insert them around design to fill space. Insert one holly berry spray above and one below plaid bow. Fold chenille stem in half and twist about two inches from folded end. Insert two ends into back top of foam and glue. Push loop up for hanger.

SPLENDID SNOWMAN STOCKING

The tradition of hanging the stockings comes from long ago. Today, there is still excitement in this tradition on Christmas Eve, as families anticipate the goodies and presents from Santa. And the friendly snowman never looked better than when surrounded by glistening crystal stars!

Materials

Red stocking

Transfer paper

Tracing paper

Pencil

Fabric paint: white, yellow, black, and glitter gold

Fabric brush

Fabric glue

10 emerald navette cabochons, 15×7mm

3 ruby faceted round stones, 7mm

13 dark sapphire faceted round stones, 7mm

7 emerald faceted round stones, 7mm

5 ruby faceted round stones, 9mm

17 crystal faceted round stones, 7mm

8 crystal faceted stars, 15mm

¼ yard satin ribbon, ⅛ inch wide

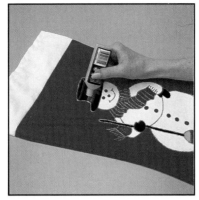

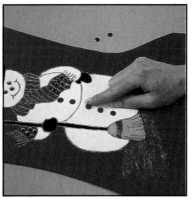

1 Adjust pattern size to fit your stocking. Trace pattern onto premade stocking. With black paint and fabric brush, paint hat (leave middle section red), mittens, and broom handle. Paint broom top and bottom yellow (leave middle section red). Paint snowman's body white. If one coat does not cover completely, apply more paint until the surface is evenly covered. Allow paint to dry (time may vary depending on type of paint used).

2 With glitter gold paint and fabric brush, lightly paint left side of hat, ribbon, scarf, and ground below snowman. Outline all shapes and draw mouth with gold. Glue emerald navette cabochons and 7mm ruby faceted stones to hat. Place three 7mm dark sapphire faceted stones on face, two for eyes and one for the nose.

3 The remaining 7mm dark sapphires and emeralds will be used on scarf ends. To right scarf end, in last four sections, starting at top row, glue dark sapphire, emerald, dark sapphire. To second row, glue three dark sapphires. To third row, glue three emeralds. To fourth row, glue dark sapphire, emerald, dark sapphire. To left scarf end, at top row, glue dark sapphire, emerald, dark sapphire. To second row, glue emerald, dark sapphire. Glue 9mm rubies as buttons.

4 Randomly glue crystal and star stones around snowman. Make a bow with ribbon; glue to broom.

FRAGRANTLY FESTIVE BASKET

Giving warms our hearts and the hearts of those we love. The gift of a handmade basket can be enjoyed for many holiday seasons to come.

Materials

White basket, medium size

1 stem glittered pine, with twelve 4-inch sections

Glue gun and glue sticks

1 yard red and green plaid ribbon, 1 inch wide

32-gauge cloth-covered wire

Wire cutters

1 stem gold glittered cedar spray, with six 4-inch sections

1 stem glittered white cedar, with eight 3-inch sections

1 shiny red berry spray, with 10 branches

4 gold jingle bells, 1¼ inches each

1 Pull 12 sections off main stem of glittered pine. Glue these pieces in a loose *L* pattern along one side and up basket handle.

2 Make a four-loop bow with three-inch loops. Secure with a two-inch length of cloth-covered wire. Set aside. Pull six sections off main stem of gold glittered cedar. Glue these to fill in pattern formed by pine pieces.

3 Pull eight sections off main stem of glittered white cedar. Glue these pieces evenly throughout design.

4 Cut berry spray into ten sections. Place berries throughout design. Glue bow made in Step 2 into center bottom of design. Apply glue to each jingle bell and place evenly around bow.

HO·HO·HO SANTA POST

"Santa Claus is comin' to town!" This folk art Santa is sure to bring a chuckle or two from young and old alike!

Materials

4 × 4 inches wood post, about 22 inches long

Handsaw

Pencil

Transparent paper

Tracing paper

Palette or palette paper

Acrylic paints: fleshtone, black, ivory, island coral, berry red, liberty blue

¾-inch flat brush

10/0 detail brush

Spray satin sealer

Glue gun and glue sticks

15 to 20 strands raffia

2 silk holly leaves plus berries

White pom-pon, 2 inches

1 Cut post to desired length. Trace pattern from book using transparent paper and pencil. With tracing paper between transparent paper (carbon side down) and post, use a pencil to draw on lines for face and hat.

2 Use ¾-inch brush to paint face area with fleshtone paint. Paint hat with berry red. Paint hat fur, hair, mustache, and beard with ivory. Use one coat so that wood shows through, giving an aged appearance.

3 Use 10/0 brush to paint detail lines of hat, hair, and mustache in black. Paint iris of eyes liberty blue and pupils and eyelashes black. Add ivory eyebrows and highlight on lower right sides of eyes. Dip brush handle into ivory and dot the top of each eye. Add nose and lines around face with black. Using a dry brush, add a light coat of island coral to cheeks and tip of nose.

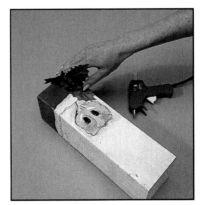

4 Spray post with satin sealer. Make a simple bow with raffia strands. Glue holly leaves and berries to top right side of hat. Glue raffia bow just above holly. Glue pom-pon to top of post.

WELL-LIT WELCOME

Colorful lights are a part

of our holiday decorating

that expresses our joy and

merriment in the season.

This swag of painted

wooden lights extends a

warm welcome to all your

visitors!

Materials

7 bulbs cut from pine stock

Scroll or band saw

Power drill

Sandpaper or sanding pads

Acrylic paints: bright red,
   liberty blue*, Christmas
   green, pumpkin, white,
   black, luscious lemon,
   metallic gold

¾-inch flat brush

10/0 detail brush

Satin sealer

6 inches rattail cord

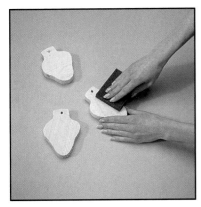

1 Cut seven bulbs from pine stock with scroll saw or band saw. Drill a 1/8-inch hole in top of each bulb. Lightly sand all bulbs.

2 Using 3/4-inch flat brush, paint two bulbs bright red, two luscious lemon, one Christmas green, one pumpkin, and one liberty blue.* Paint tops of each bulb metallic gold. Let dry.

3 Use 10/0 detail brush to add detail lines to each bulb, including letters. Use white paint to make a comma stroke in upper left of each bulb. Brush on satin sealer. Let dry.

4 String rattail cord through W bulb and tie a knot at top of bulb; leave a few inches of tail to left. Repeat with each bulb, leaving about two inches of cord between bulbs.

*For photographic reasons, we substituted a second pumpkin bulb for the liberty blue.

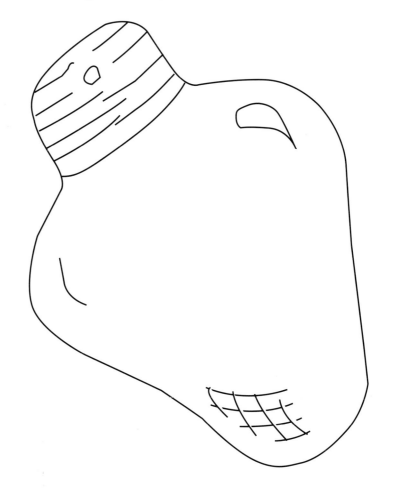

POINSETTIA PLACE SETTINGS

Poinsettias, the traditional Christmas flower, embellish this festive place setting. Would you believe a potato and some paint were all that was needed to achieve these results? Just cut a potato and watch your creativity bloom! Then to top your place setting off, make a napkin ring to complement your designs.

Materials

White placemats

Napkins

Iron

4 large potatoes

Large knife

Sharp pencil

Craft knife

Fabric paints: yellow light, lacquer red, medium green, diamond yellow, sparkling ruby, lime green, yellow

3 flat brushes, ¾ inch each

Palette or palette paper

Scratch paper for practice

6 inches red bendable ribbon for each ring, ¾ inch wide

Scissors

Glue gun and glue sticks

Silk holly sprigs with berries

1 Wash and dry placemats and napkins. Press. Use large knife to slice potatoes in half lengthwise for flowers and large leaf shapes; in half widthwise for small ones. Draw design on potato with pencil before carving with craft knife. Trim edges down. After you've carved a basic leaf shape, cut a center line with lines slanting upward on either side of center. Cut three to five leaf shapes, and two flowers. Carve several small circles in the center of each flower.

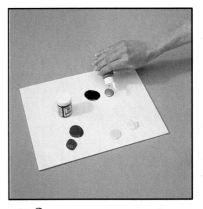

2 Squeeze or scoop paints onto palette. Colors will be mixed as you apply them to carved potatoes. The poinsettias are lacquer red and sparkling ruby. Flower centers are yellow light and diamond yellow. Leaves are medium green and lime green. Do not dilute paints. Use a different brush for each color group.

4 Paint poinsettia. Place potato on a corner of placemat and press onto fabric; carefully lift up placemat and rub underside to help paint transfer. Lift potato; touch up areas that didn't print with a paintbrush.

3 Dry potatoes. Use a brush to apply paint, then press onto scratch paper. If you aren't happy, recut it or try again on a fresh potato.

5 Next, paint a large leaf: half with lime green, the other half with medium green. Add a few brush strokes of contrasting green on either side, in same direction as veins. Place leaf next to flower on placemat; press to transfer. Before repainting stamp, restamp to create a lighter, background stamp that fills in white space around flower. Add more leaves of various sizes around flower.

6 After surrounding first poinsettia with leaves, add another red blossom and surround it with leaves. Work your way around placemat in this manner, always filling in leaves before printing another blossom. Alternate poinsettia stamps as you move around placemat, as well as turning them in different directions for variety. Do the same for leaves, especially when they fall side by side. Avoid symmetry. As you work, turn placemat around to see it from different angles.

7 To cover little holes of white, use a leaf stamp with little paint and lightly press on a spot to fill in with a background leaf. For edges, print a few leaves half on and half off placemat. Use yellow paint to add small raised dots in center of each poinsettia.

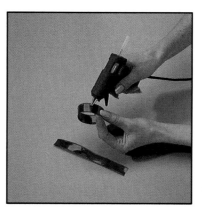

8 To print napkin, work as you did on placemat. The paints used on this project do not require heat setting. Wait 48 hours before laundering.

9 For napkin rings: Hot glue ribbon ends together.

10 Glue holly sprig over joint, pointing up. Glue another sprig on top of first, pointing in opposite direction.

 BASKET OF CHRISTMAS

Apples and spice and everything nice are the ingredients for this tabletop arrangement. Festive plaid ribbon, bells, and delightful packages are nestled into the branches of the tree. You make cinnamon ornaments to hang—why not make extras for your larger tree? What a very merry accent for a very Merry Christmas!

Materials

Red bushel basket, about 9 inches around and 7 inches tall

Glue gun and glue sticks

Cloth-covered wire

3⅓ yards plaid ribbon, 1½ inches wide

10 glittered plastic pine sprigs, 3 inches long each

16 assorted Christmas packages, about 1½ inches each

Novelty Santa

1½ yards green satin ribbon, ⅛ inch wide

7 gold jingle bells, ⅞ inch each

2⅔ yards red satin ribbon, ⅛ inch wide

36 cinnamon sticks, 2½ inches long

18 red lacquered apples, ⅞ inch each

Tabletop Christmas tree, 24 inches tall

18 ornaments with bow and two jingle bells, ¾ inch

1 Cut a two-yard length of plaid ribbon and secure with wire. Make an eight-loop bow, each loop measuring three inches with 12-inch streamers. Glue bow to top edge of basket. Drape and glue streamers about two inches from bottom of basket.

2 Glue glittered pine sprigs around top edge of basket. Slightly overlap sprigs.

3 Glue a package in middle of bow and the rest around top edge of basket. Glue Santa to basket edge, just right of bow.

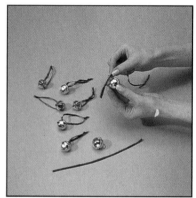

4 Cut one 6-inch length, five 8-inch lengths, and one 10-inch length of green ribbon. Tie a jingle bell to each length of ribbon by looping ribbon through hole in top of bell, bringing ends together and tying.

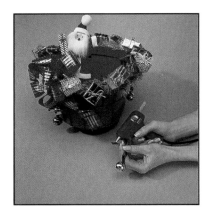

5 Glue three bells in a cluster under center bow on basket. Glue the other four equally spaced around outside of basket.

6 To decorate the tree: Form ornaments by gluing three cinnamon sticks together. Cut twelve 8-inch lengths of red ribbon. Glue middle of ribbon onto cluster of cinnamon sticks. Bring ribbon ends together and tie a knot.

7 Glue red apples, bell and bow ornaments, and cinnamon stick ornaments to tree branches.

8 Form an eight-loop bow with remaining plaid ribbon. Each loop should measure 2½ inches. Attach to top of tree with wire. Insert decorated tree into basket.

YULETIDE COASTERS

Protect your tables and decorate your home with these fun and easy plastic canvas coasters. Stitched in no time, you can make them for your home and give them as gifts to special friends!

Materials

⅓ sheet plastic canvas, #7 mesh

#16 tapestry needle

Worsted weight yarn:
  White—20 yards
  Red—5 yards
  Green—4 yards
  Yellow—1 yard

4 acrylic coasters

Instructions:

Cut four pieces of canvas 19 holes × 19 holes. Trim according to dark outer lines of charts.

Stitch pieces following charts, noting that most is worked in continental stitch. The green portions of large package are cross-stitched. Back-stitch bows on wreath, bell, and large gift. Work holly berries, poinsettia center, clapper on bell, and knots on bows in French knots. Work poinsettia in long straight stitches, noting direction of stitches. Overcast all edges in white.

Before mounting coasters, discard foam inserts. Peel adhesive backing from a styrene piece from coaster, and lay finished coaster on top, centering carefully. Insert into an acrylic coaster, pressing to secure. Repeat with other three coasters.

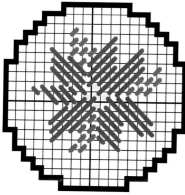

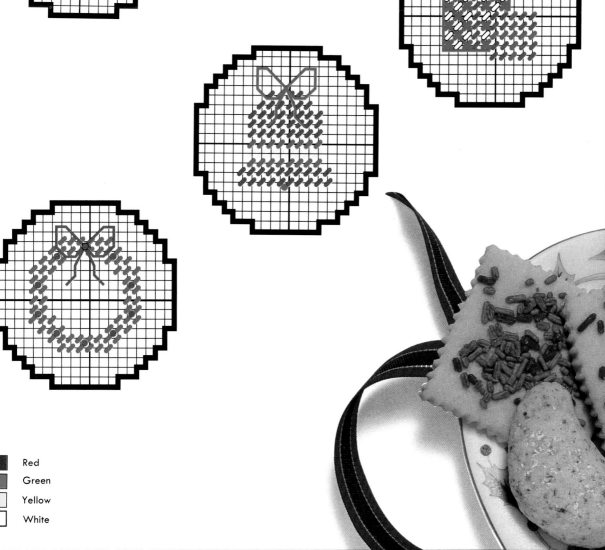

■	Red
▨	Green
▫	Yellow
□	White

CHRISTMAS CHEER MUGS

A unique way to preserve the warm greetings of the holiday is to encase your needlework inside a plastic mug. Hot chocolate never tasted better!

Materials

2 red mugs (with vinyl weave inserts)

#24 tapestry needle

Floss: red, green

Scissors

Instructions:

Cross-stitch with three of six strands of floss. Take mug apart and remove vinyl weave strip. Find center horizontally and vertically and mark with a pin or needle. Find center of chart by using arrows to determine where to begin stitching.

For second mug, insert Joy in place of Noel. When stitching is completed, insert vinyl weave back into mug, placing seams next to handle area. Snap insert back into mug.

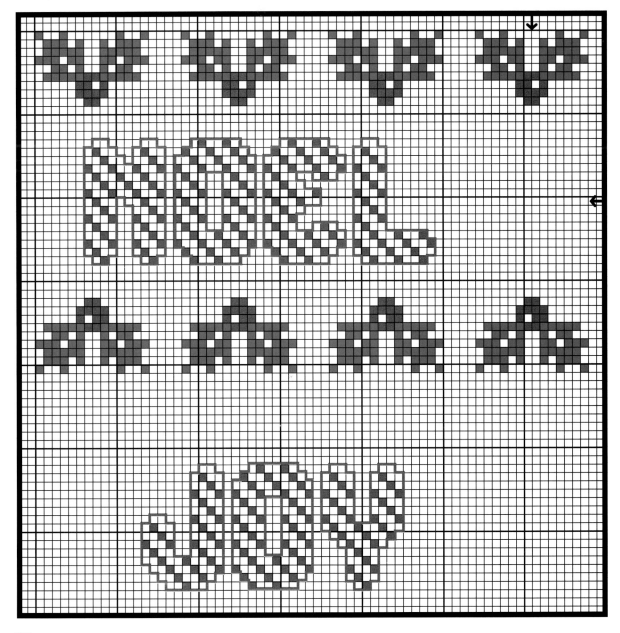

■ Red
■ Green

SHIMMERING SNOWFLAKE WREATH

Sheer white ribbon woven through pine boughs, gold pinecones, and glittering snowflakes remind us of the beauty of a picture-perfect white Christmas— even on the warmest holiday morning!

Materials

20 pinecones, 2 inches each

Gold metallic spray

Glue gun and glue

Pine wreath, 20 inches wide

5 yards white/gold sheer wired ribbon with gold stars, 3 inches wide

Scissors

Cloth-covered wire

Wire cutters

10 plastic frosted snowflakes, 4 inches each

2⅓ yards of gold metallic tubing, ⅜ inches wide

1 Spray pinecones with gold spray. Allow to dry. Apply glue to each pinecone and position throughout wreath.

2 Form an eight-loop bow with the sheer wired ribbon. Each loop should measure 3½ inches. Cut off remaining ribbon. Secure bow with cloth-covered wire. Wire the bow onto the wreath, securing with extra wire.

3 Drape remaining ribbon around wreath, using wired pine branches to wrap around ribbon and hold in place.

4 Apply a small amount of glue to one tip of each snowflake and place around wreath.

5 Cut metallic tubing into 12-inch lengths. Form two loops with each length and secure with cloth-covered wire. Trim excess wire. Glue these throughout design.

CREATIVE CANDY WREATH

A luscious wreath filled with sugarplums for all the good little girls and boys, young and old, to enjoy. Confections are one of the delights of the Christmas season—they can be decorative and delicious!

Materials

1-inch straight pins

Tacky glue

Plastic foam wreath, 12 inches around

9 yards Christmas ribbon, 2½ inches wide

Stapler and staples

Red peppermint candies

8 yards each red, green, silver, and gold metallic curling ribbon, ¼ inch wide

Cloth-covered wire

1 Dip all pins into glue before inserting into wreath. Secure one end of Christmas ribbon to back of foam wreath with a few straight pins. Tightly wrap wreath with ribbon to completely cover. Trim excess ribbon.

2 Use remainder of Christmas ribbon and form box pleats around outside back of wreath. Staple pleats to hold. Pin pleats in place around wreath back.

3 Secure candy to wreath with straight pins dipped in glue. (If you wish people to eat the candy, don't dip pins into glue.) Equally space candy along wreath.

4 Cut six 1-yard lengths of each red, green, silver, and gold curling ribbons. Form each length into a six-loop bow with loops measuring 1¹/₂ inches, securing with wire. Secure each to wreath with pins. Use the bows to fill in space around candy.

5 Cut remaining curling ribbon into six-inch lengths, curl and tie onto ends of candies randomly throughout design.

SNOWFLAKE WRAPPING PAPER

The delicate pattern of snowflakes will generate a blizzard of compliments! Once you've cut out the snowflakes, you can make many different versions— think of all the possibilities.

Materials

12 to 15 squares of paper, about 4½ square inches

Scissors

Iron

White paper

Plastic snowflakes (optional)

Blue spray paint

1 Start with a square of paper. Fold bottom edge of your square up to top edge to make a rectangle. Fold this rectangle in half so you have a square. Fold this square from corner to corner to create a triangle.

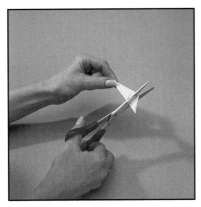

2 With the single fold at the bottom, fold down side with several creases to touch bottom edge. Cut off the paper that hangs off the end.

3 Now you're ready to cut designs in the paper with the scissors. Some designs can be cut on the side with the single fold, but don't cut it away completely or snowflake will fall apart. Experiment with cutting out diamonds, circles, and odd shapes from the multicreased side. Unfold paper. Cut 12 to 15 snowflakes. Iron them so they lie flat. Iron sheets of white paper.

4 In a well-ventilated area, arrange snowflakes on white paper so they overlap slightly. If you have plastic snowflakes, use them to weigh down paper ones.

5 Shake can of paint well before spraying lightly over paper, using a gentle back and forth motion. Hold can high off paper, and spray directly above to avoid moving snowflakes. Allow to dry for a few minutes so you don't smudge paint when you remove snowflakes. Snowflakes can be reused.

DANCING GINGERBREAD TREE SKIRT

Sweet confections border a tree skirt. Gingerbread boys, candy canes, and holly leaves are ironed on—a perfect complement to a lovely Christmas tree!

Materials

1 yard red felt

Chalk

String

Iron

1 yard fusible adhesive

¼ yard washable green satin

⅓ yard brown imitation suede

¼ yard mini-print Christmas fabric

Scissors

Fabric paints: copper glitter, green shiny, pearl, red shiny, black shiny

Fabric glitter: medium, fine

1 yard Christmas ribbon

3 safety pins

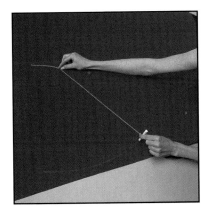

1 Chalk a 34-inch circle on felt material.

2 Iron adhesive to back of material. On medium setting, place iron on paper side of adhesive and press for three to five seconds. Trace patterns on paper back of prepared materials. Use green for 17 holly leaves. Use brown for eight small and six large gingerbread boys. Use mini-print for 15 candy canes. Cut out and peel paper off pieces.

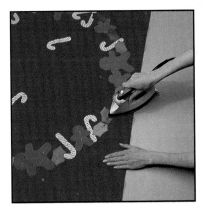

3 Position gingerbread, holly, and candy canes around chalk edge. Place three candy canes between center and border. Iron appliqués to felt; let cool. Be sure all edges are secured. Reiron if necessary, but do not overheat (iron three to seven seconds only).

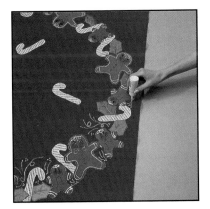

4 Rest tip of fabric paint bottle on appliqué/felt edge and outline each piece. Outline holly with green, gingerbread with copper glitter, and candy cane with pearl. Add detail lines to center of holly and stripe on candy canes. Dry brush gingerbread cheeks red and add facial features in black. Finish icing detail with pearl, buttons and bows with red and green (follow picture). Use pearl paint to add curly stems and dots to fill in noticeable spaces in border. Sprinkle glitter (medium and fine) over wet fabric paint.

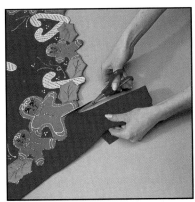

5 Let dry, then shake off excess glitter. Cut away excess felt, leaving a scalloped edge. Cut line should be close to but not cutting into paint.

6 Draw and cut a line from center to rear break on border design. Cut out a 2½-inch circle in center for tree. Make bows for center candy canes and safety pin from underneath.

NOEL CROSS-STITCH ORNAMENTS

Every year we like to add

new ornaments to our

Christmas tree collection.

Beautifully stitched

ornaments, such as these

cross-stitch ones, are

especially appealing!

Materials

1 yard white cross-stitch cloth, #14 count

#24 tapestry needle

Floss: yellow, orange, pink, red, burgundy, emerald, forest, purple, ivory, light tan, black, dark red, tan, brown

Scissors

Adhesive-backed mounting board

Glue gun and glue sticks

4 yards red gathered ribbon

1 yard red satin ribbon, ⅛ inch wide

1 square green felt (optional)

Instructions:

Stitch according to printed charts and instructions. To finish: Trim cross-stitching to desired shapes and sizes. Cut pieces of adhesive-backed mounting board to match shapes. Affix cross-stitching to mounting board backings. Using a glue gun or thick white craft glue and starting at the bottom center of each design, carefully glue the ribbon around the outside edge of each design, slightly overlapping at the bottom. Make a loop from eight inches red satin ribbon, and glue to top back side of each piece for a hanger. If desired, cut pieces of green felt to cover backs of ornaments, gluing them in place.

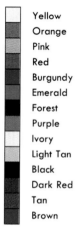

Yellow
Orange
Pink
Red
Burgundy
Emerald
Forest
Purple
Ivory
Light Tan
Black
Dark Red
Tan
Brown

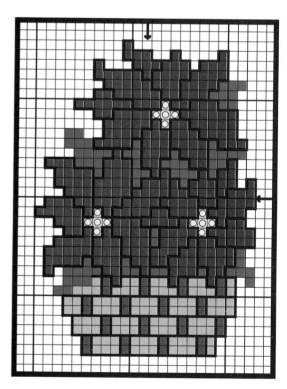

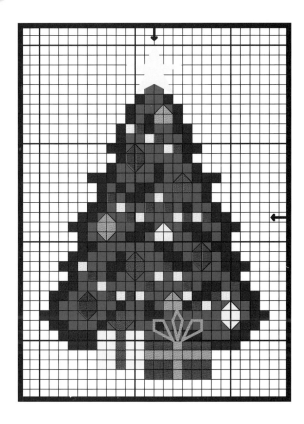

FAMILY FUN PROJECT

Clay ornaments can be a fun family project—and easy enough for a child. Once Mom or Dad bakes them, they'll last forever!

Materials

Waxed paper

Polymer clay: 2 packages brown, 1 red, 1 white, 2 green, 2 bronze, 1 yellow

Transparent paper

Pencil

Rolling pin

Craft knife

Paper clips (for hangers)

Wire cutters

Cookie sheet (nonconducting surface)

Metal spatula

Brown paper bags

Paintbrush

Varnish (for modeling compounds)

Red and white ribbon, 1/8 inch wide (optional)

General information: Cover your work surface with waxed paper. Work with lightest color first; darker colors stain. Work the clay in your hands to soften it, then roll it into a coil. Do the same with the other colors needed.

1 For holly ornament: Twine green and bronze coils together and fold them back on themselves, twisting the new coil until you have a marbled pattern.

4 To make a metal hanger for holly and gingerbread man, partially unbend a paper clip and cut off all but 1/2-inch loop. Poke this into the top of ornament.

2 Roll coil flat. When it's 1/4 to 1/8 inch thick, use holly pattern and craft knife to make two leaves. Lightly score surfaces. Press leaf tops together.

5 Bake on a non-conducting surface (slate or Pyrex®) in a 250 degree oven for 15 to 30 minutes. Clay will be soft when hot; it hardens as it cools. Ventilate kitchen when baking. Do not overbake; fumes could be toxic. Remove ornaments with spatula and place on brown paper bag. (Keep cookie utensils for clay only!) Once the ornament is cool, brush on varnish. Glue a ribbon on candy canes for hangers and a bow to holly.

3 From red coil, pull off three small pieces for berries. Roll them into pea-sized balls. Push berries gently onto tops of leaves.

1 For candy cane: See general information. Roll out the coils until long and thin. Cut white coil in half, then cut red coils to same length. Layer white and red, then red and white on top.

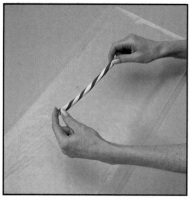

2 Gently roll colors together to form one large roll. Roll should be about 1/2 inch thick. Trim ends and twist so colors spiral. Bend head to form candy cane shape. (Go to Step 5.)

1 For gingerbread man: See general information. Use rolling pin to flatten brown clay to 1/4 inch thick. Make a gingerbread man using pattern; cut around edges with craft knife.

2 Roll bits of yellow, red, and green clay into small balls (pea sized) for buttons. Roll two small white balls for eyes, flatten slightly. Press a bit of green into middle of white. Roll out small pieces of yellow, red, and green for rickrack. With a craft knife, cut a zigzag pattern and place on arms, legs, and neck. Roll a thin red tube for mouth. (Go to Step 4.)

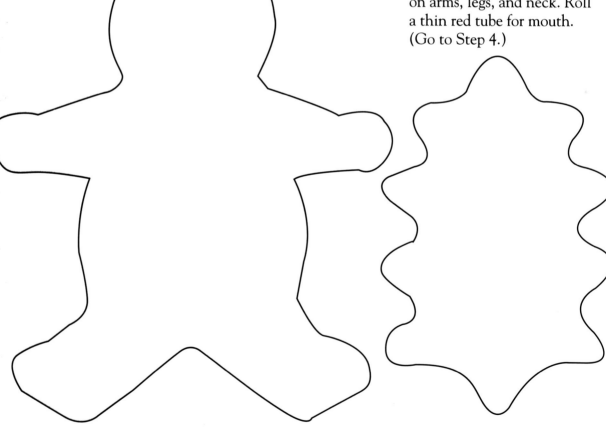

Handmade CHRISTMAS *Ornaments*

Designer and Contributing Writer
Jane Johnston

Publications International, Ltd.

Photography:
Sacco Productions Limited/Chicago

Photographers:
Ken Hyne, Tom O'Connell, Peter Ross

Photo Stylists:
Linda Banach, Paula Walters

Photo Production:
Roberta Ellis
Models/Royal Model Mangement:
Theresa Lesniak, Monica Magdziak

Jane Johnston is a crafts designer who obtained her Bachelor of Arts degree in Studio Arts from the University of Pittsburgh. She has supplied many handmade Christmas ornaments to retail stores throughout southwestern Pennsylvania. Ms. Johnston is also a member of the Craftsman's Guild of Pittsburgh.

CONTENTS

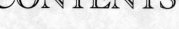

INTRODUCTION:

VICTORIAN THEME TREE

TEXAS THEME TREE

CHILDREN'S THEME TREE

COUNTRY THEME TREE

INTRODUCTION: STEPS TO SUCCESS

Crafting handmade Christmas ornaments can be great family fun or an exciting activity for friends of all ages to enjoy. Making your own ornaments can help put the warmth and heart back into a season that, for some, has become "too much." The gift of a handmade ornament says you care enough to spend time on someone special. Give a child an ornament that you have made, and he or she will remember you every time the ornament is hung on a Christmas tree in years to come. For a little something special to give to your friends and neighbors, a handmade ornament is just the right gift.

SOME BASIC TOOLS

Glue. In most cases, white craft glue and hot glue guns can be used interchangeably, but there are differences. White glue takes longer to set up, or establish a bond. Hot glue is better if you don't want to hold something in place for a long time or if you don't want to wait between steps while the glue dries. However, white glue bonds better than hot glue on surfaces that are nonporous (such as a button surface); white glue also bonds better when gluing dissimilar surfaces (nonporous buttons to a porous grapevine).

Since hot glue comes out of the gun in a glob, often some glue will show around the edges of the glued object. In this instance, use a sharp knife or a single-edge razor blade to trim off the excess. By contrast, white glue dries transparent, unless you use extremely large amounts.

When you buy a hot glue gun, consider getting a trigger-action mini gun. Mini guns deliver the smallest amount of glue possible and offer the best control of the nozzle. When using a hot glue gun, let the glue completely cool before getting rid of the annoying "strings" that often appear between the ornament and the hot glue gun. Finally, let the glue cool completely before releasing the glued object; otherwise, the object may shift position.

When you buy white glue, chose one that dries transparent and is specifically made for crafts. The white glue should be flexible, which is an important feature when you are gluing fabric.

Scissors. Although scissors are usually not mentioned in the lists of "What You'll Need," they are necessary for preparing almost every project. Be sure your scissors are sharp; otherwise, cutting felt and polyester batting will be difficult. If possible, try to have one special pair of scissors for cutting fabrics only. Cutting hair or paper dulls the blades quickly.

Orange sticks and toothpicks. An orange stick (from your manicuring kit) is useful for setting rhinestones. With rhinestones or any of the variety of studs available, the main action is pushing the points on the settings through the material and then bending the points over. Although an orange stick takes a bit longer than a setting machine, it will save you money. Toothpicks are useful for almost every project. Toothpicks can be used to spread glue around, to hold things in place, or to push small objects around.

Tweezers. Tweezers are another handy item to keep with your craft tools. They can be used to pick up small objects, such as goggle eyes.

Batting. For felt ornaments, use batting instead of stuffing. Stuffing often develops clumps, especially when it is being pushed into something. Stuffing also never seems to get into the far corners of the ornament.

Paper twist. Paper twist comes in a variety of widths, depending on the manufacturer. Adjust the directions of a project to reflect different widths. Do not cut the paper twist to the size specified in the directions until you have unraveled and spread it as flat as possible.

HANDY TECHNIQUES

Glue. Whenever you are gluing something, it is better to put the glue on the object to be placed (if possible) rather than on the surface where the object will end up. This provides better control and prevents the glue from being smeared.

After cutting the stem from a ribbon rose, apply a dab of hot glue to the rear of the flower. The glue will hold the rose together.

If you are gluing something with a stem, first trim the stem to ¼ inch. Apply glue to the ¼-inch stem by sticking the stem down the nozzle of the hot glue gun.

To make leaves appear more realistic, apply glue to the bottom rear of the leaves only. This will make them stand up and appear lifelike.

To make it look as if there are more flowers, fruit, gift packages, or bears than actually used, glue the first round of items just peeking above the edge of the object (for example, a sleigh or a cornucopia). Glue the second row to the first row at a slightly higher level. Glue the third row to the second at an even higher level. Make sure there are no holes where someone can see down into the hollow mound you've created.

Ribbon. When choosing a wide ribbon for a bigger project (such as a tree garland), use ribbon with wire in the edge. The wire will help give the ribbon a more graceful line.

If you can't find the ribbon you want in a narrow width, buy wider ribbon and cut it to the width you want.

Beads. Strings of beads usually come with about 6 inches of extra string on either end. To cut a string of beads, make a knot at one end of the string that is large enough that the beads cannot slip off. Move as many inches of beads as you need down against this knot. Tie another knot just past the last bead and cut the string. Place a dab of white glue on each knot to prevent unraveling. (To knot a string in a specific spot, first make a loose knot around a straight pin. Then move the pin to the spot where you want the knot. Tighten the string.)

SOME GENERAL DIRECTIONS

Several directions apply to several projects: making loopy bows, cutting patterns, or tying various knots.

To make a loopy bow:

1. Cut the ribbon to the specified length.

2. Find an object that is approximately the same diameter as the loop of the bow. (Your fingers can work well for this: one for a small loop, two for a larger loop.)

3. Leaving about 1 inch free, wrap the ribbon around the object. Leave another inch free at the end. Cross the two free ends over the loop.

4. Insert a smaller piece of ribbon through all the loops; bring around and tie in a knot.

5. Pull the bow from the object and separate the loops in an attractive arrangement.

To cut out patterns:

1. Place tracing paper over the pattern. Using a pen or pencil, trace the pattern onto the paper.

2. Using rubber cement, bond the tracing paper to a piece of thin cardboard.

3. Cut the shape out, following the traced lines.

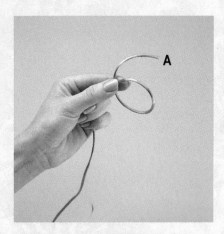

To tie an overhand knot:

1. Create a loop with your line. Note point A.

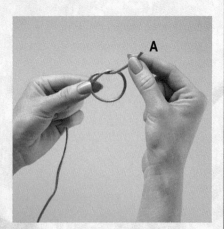

2. Pass point A around and through the loop from behind.

3. Pull the line tight.

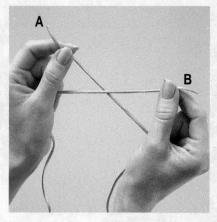

To tie a square knot:

1. Take the two ends of your line, one in each hand. Pass point B over point A.

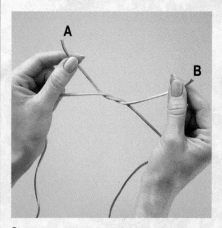

2. Wrap point B around point A, bringing it underneath, up, and out.

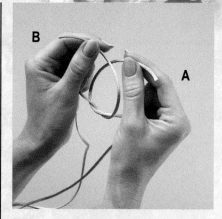

3. Pass point B over point A, forming a loop.

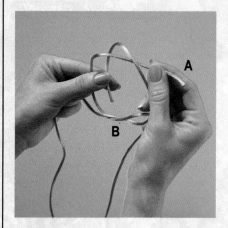

4. Bring point B under point A, then through the loop and out.

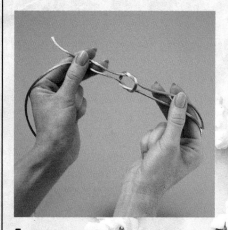

5. Pull the line tight with both hands.

THEME TREE IDEAS

Once you've created ornaments for a theme tree, you'll need to think about tree skirts, garlands, and tree toppers to finish decorating your tree.

Victorian Theme Tree. For a tree skirt you can use an old set of lacy curtains. For garlands try 3-inch-wide lace gathered with a bow every 2 to 3 feet. Another option is 3-inch-wide ribbon in a pale color with wire in the edges. A ball of dried or silk flowers with ribbon trailers works well as a tree topper.

Texas Theme Tree. A tree skirt can be made from red and blue bandannas stitched together, or use 3 yards of burlap or cowboy theme fabric. For a garland use several strands of jute twine gathered in a bow every two feet. Small American flags stuck into the sides of the bows might look nice. An alternative garland can be made from bandannas tied together into a string. Make a large star from lightweight aluminum or stitched from burlap to serve as a tree topper.

Children's Theme Tree. Instead of a tree skirt, try piling small stuffed animals around the base of the tree; or, a length of brightly colored flannel would make a fun tree skirt. Use candy for the garland: a string of cellophane-wrapped gumballs or thick red yarn with candy canes tied in every two feet. A tree topper could be created with a loopy bow made from thick red yarn.

Country Theme Tree. For a tree skirt, start with a 3-yard piece of muslin or brown butcher's paper. Next, cut potato stamps in basic shapes and then stamp the material using acrylic paint. A strand of jute twine works well as a garland. Gather the twine in a bow every two feet; stick bright red berries or a holly pick in each side of the bow. You can also use jute twine to make the tree topper: Make a thick loopy bow from the twine.

HOW DIFFICULT IS EACH ORNAMENT?

The ornament projects vary in difficulty. Many are easy; many are intermediate; and some are difficult. Most of the projects have been designed to be as simple as possible. The easy projects are best suited for beginners. The intermediate and difficult projects use many of the same skills called for in the easy projects, but there are more steps and more parts to put together.

Victorian Theme Tree
Beaded Wreath: easy
Cornucopia of Roses: easy
Hats Off to the Holidays: easy
Royal Yule Ornament: intermediate
Snow Bird: intermediate
Victorian Angel: difficult

Texas Theme Tree
Festive Bolo: easy
Holly Badge: easy
Pepper Yule Party: easy
Red-Hot Wreath: easy
Cowgirl Hat: intermediate
Christmas Kerchief: intermediate
On the Christmas Trail: intermediate
Texas Santa: intermediate

Children's Theme Tree
Bears on a Sleigh Ride: easy
Christmas Olé: easy
Pom-Pom Snowman: easy
Dinosaur in December: intermediate
Noel Rocking Horse: intermediate

Country Theme Tree
Buttons 'n' Eyelet Wreath: easy
Old-Fashioned Buttermold: easy
Country Christmas Goose: intermediate
Holiday Holstein: intermediate
Jute Twist: intermediate
Old World St. Nick: difficult

Individual Ornaments
And a Partridge in a...: easy
Braided Candy Cane: easy
Dove of Peace: easy
Joy to the World: easy
Santa's Sleigh: easy
Angel of the Vine: intermediate
Cross-Stitch Christmas: intermediate
O Christmas Tree!: intermediate
Bountiful Santa: difficult
Button-Down Santa: difficult
Jolly Clay Santa: difficult
Yuletide Bauble: difficult

VICTORIAN
THEME
TREE

Imagine yourself
in an earlier time; catch
the feeling
of Christmas past
with a Victorian
theme tree.
Cornucopias, lace,
and pastels will bring
the look and feel
of this refined era
to all your Christmas
celebrations. Turn to
the Introduction for
ideas on Victorian
garlands,
skirts, and topppers.

Royal Yule Ornament

1. Cut out the pattern. See page 64 for the "Royal Yule Ornament" pattern. See Introduction, page 5, for directions on cutting out patterns. Cut, on the bias, 7 pattern pieces from the blue fabric.

2. Attach the 7 pieces of fabric to the foam ball with pins. The pieces should be evenly distributed around the ball and overlap slightly.

3. Cover the overlapping fabric edges with the 7 lengths of gold trim. Secure with pins and spot glue in place. Remove the pins after the glue has dried.

4. Glue a 3½-inch length of gold trim in a circle to the top of the ball and another to the bottom.

5. Glue the tassel to the center of the bottom circle of gold trim.

6. Place the 24-inch length of blue ribbon on top of the 24-inch length of gold ribbon. Make a 1-inch-diameter loopy bow. Tie off the bow with the 8-inch length of blue ribbon. (See Introduction, page 5, for instructions on making a loopy bow.) Glue the bow to the center of the top circle of gold trim.

7. Fold the 8-inch length of gold ribbon in half and tie an overhand knot near the open end. Glue the folded end near the loopy bow.

What You'll Need

12-inch-square blue fabric
Scissors
3-inch-diameter foam ball
Sequin pins
7 lengths antique gold trim,
4¾ inches each
Hot glue mini gun
2 lengths antique gold trim,
3½ inches each
5-inch gold tinsel tassel
24 inches blue ⅛-inch ribbon
24 inches gold ⅛-inch ribbon
8 inches blue ⅛-inch ribbon
8 inches gold ⅛-inch ribbon

Tips and Variations

Give this ornament a Texas or Western look by using a bandanna for the material. Use jute twine for the trim and tassel.

5. Lay the 18-inch lengths of ribbon on top of each other. Make a 2-inch bow and glue it to the lower side of the open end of the cone, just below the flower arrangement.

6. Fold the 12-inch length of ribbon in half. Make an overhand knot near the open end. Glue the folded end just below the 2-inch bow.

1. Starting at the lowest point of the mouth of the cone, weave the 9-inch length of $1/16$-inch ribbon around the edge. Trim any excess ribbon and glue the ends in place.

2. Mix together the light and dark mauve rosebuds. Twist the stems together and, about 2 inches from the bottom of the flowers, bend the stems back on themselves. If necessary, clip the stems to a total length of 3 inches.

3. Insert arrangement into cone. Glue one rose on each side and top and bottom to edge of cone.

TIPS AND VARIATIONS

For variety, use miniature poinsettias in pastel colors.

WHAT YOU'LL NEED

5-inch crochet cone

9 inches $1/16$-inch mauve ribbon

Scissors

Hot glue mini gun

1 bunch (6 flowers) $3/4$-inch dark mauve, brushed gold rosebuds

1 bunch (6 flowers) $3/4$-inch light mauve, brushed gold rosebuds

Wire cutters

9 rose leaves, $1/2$-inch leaves

3 lengths $1/16$-inch mauve ribbon, 18 inches each

12 inches $1/16$-inch mauve ribbon

4. Clip the stems from the rose leaves. One at a time, apply glue to the bottom of the leaves and insert them into the flower bouquet in an attractive arrangement.

1. Glue the 8-mm beads around base of crown of the crochet hat.

2. Clip the wires off the glass ball picks. Glue the picks in a clump of three at the crown's base, next to the 8-mm beads.

3. Clip the stems from the leaves. Glue the leaves in an attractive arrangement next to the glass picks.

4. Make a ¾-inch-diameter loopy bow from one 15-inch length of mauve ribbon. Tie off the loopy bow with the second length of 15-inch mauve ribbon. Trim ends. (See Introduction, page 5, for instructions on making a loopy bow.) Glue the bow to the glass picks.

5. Fold the 20-inch length of ribbon in half. Insert it through the edge of the hat brim almost opposite to the glass picks. Tie an overhand knot near the end.

TIPS AND VARIATIONS

Ribbon roses could be used in place of the beads, with larger roses in place of the glass ball picks.

WHAT YOU'LL NEED

4-inch crochet hat
22 clear beads, 8 mm each
Hot glue mini gun
Wire cutters
3 glass ball picks, 15 mm each
2 rose leaves, ½ inch each
2 lengths mauve ⅛-inch ribbon,
15 inches each
20 inches mauve ¹⁄₁₆-inch ribbon

WHAT YOU'LL NEED

3½-inch wicker bird cage
Paring knife
5-inch string blue 3-mm beads
Tweezers
Hot glue mini gun
2-inch dove
Wire cutters
White craft glue
5½ inches ½-inch lace
4 inches ½-inch lace
4 inches blue ⅛-inch ribbon
8½ inches ½-inch lace
8½ inches blue ⅛-inch ribbon
2 lengths blue ⅛-inch ribbon,
18 inches each

1. Remove the tape from the bottom of the cage. Slip knife between the cage bottom and edge. Pop out the bottom.

2. Pick up one end of the bead string with tweezers. Apply hot glue to the last bead. Reach inside the cage and hold that bead against the center top of the cage until the glue dries. Repeat with the other end of the bead string.

3. Clip off the wires that stick out from the bottom of the bird. Prop the cage partially upright and hot glue the bird to the middle of the bead string. (Use tweezers to hold the bead string still.)

4. Pop the cage bottom back into place.

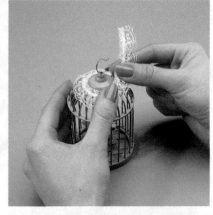

5. Apply a thin line of white glue to the back upper edge of the 5½-inch length of lace. Place the lace on the wicker bars of the cage just below the solid piece of wood at the cage's top. Trim the lace to overlap ¼ inch. Let dry.

6. Apply a thin line of white glue to the edge of the solid piece of wood above the lace from step 5 at the cage's top. Place the 4-inch length of lace around this edge. Trim the lace to overlap ¼ inch. Let dry.

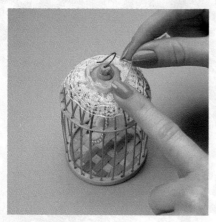

7. Apply a thin line of white glue to the upper edge of the lace from step 6. Place the 4-inch length of blue ribbon over the glue. Trim any extra ribbon.

8. Locate the solid piece of wood through which the bars pass (about 2½ inches from the bottom of the cage). Apply a thin line of white glue to this piece. Attach the 8½-inch length of lace here. Trim the lace to overlap ¼ inch. Let dry.

9. Apply a thin line of white glue to the upper edge of the lace from step 8. Place the 8½-inch length of blue ribbon over the glue. Trim any extra ribbon.

10. Lay the 18-inch lengths of ribbon on top of each other. Make a 2-inch bow. Hot glue the bow to the cage's top, at the bottom of the hook.

TIPS AND VARIATIONS

Fill the cage with a bouquet of silk rosebuds instead of a bird.

VICTORIAN ANGEL

WHAT YOU'LL NEED

3 lengths pale blue 3½-inch-wide paper twist for under-skirt and under-blouse, 3 inches each

3 lengths 3½-inch-wide pattern paper twist for over-skirt and over-blouse, 3 inches each

12 inches 3½-inch-wide pattern paper twist for wings

Hot glue mini gun

Scissors

1-inch-diameter wooden angel head

Wood wool

3 lengths off-white ⅛-inch ribbon, 18 inches each

18 inches pale blue ⅛-inch ribbon

6 inches off-white ⅛-inch ribbon

8 inches pale blue ⅛-inch ribbon

1. Untwist and flatten all paper twist.

UNDER-SKIRT AND OVER-SKIRT:

1. Run a thin line of glue down the right 3-inch side of one of the pieces of pale blue paper. Place the left 3-inch side of a second piece of pale blue paper over the glue of the first piece of pale blue paper, creating a 3-inch by 7½-inch rectangle.

2. Run a thin line of glue down the left 3-inch side of the rectangle. Bend the right 3-inch side of the rectangle around to overlap the glue line, forming a tube.

3. Gather together one end of the tube. Apply glue to the gathered end, forming a cone. This is the under-skirt.

4. To start making the over-skirt, round off the corners of a 3-inch side of 2 of the 3-inch pieces of pattern paper twist.

5. Gather together the square corners of each pattern piece. Glue the gathered end of each pattern piece to opposite sides of the top of the under-skirt. Be sure the squared ends of the two pattern pieces overlap.

UNDER-BLOUSE AND OVER-BLOUSE:

1. Run a thin line of glue down both 3½-inch sides of the third piece of pale blue paper. (This will be the under-blouse.) Place the third pattern piece of paper on top of the blue paper, pattern side up. (This will be the over-blouse.)

2. Fold the under-blouse and over-blouse in half, bringing the glued sides together. The pattern piece (over-blouse) should be on top.

3. Gather the glued sides together. Apply glue to the gathered end.

ANGEL'S BODY:

1. To join the skirt and blouse, apply glue to the tip of the skirt. Place the gathered end of the blouse on the glue and hold until the glue cools.

2. Pull the pale blue paper of the shoulders out further than the pattern paper. Be sure the shoulders are rolled, not folded.

3. Glue the angel's head to the center of the shoulders.

4. Mold a 2-inch-diameter clump of wood wool to a hair shape.

5. Apply glue to the hair area of the head. Attach the wood wool to the head.

6. To make the belt, fold 2 lengths of the 18-inch off-white ribbon in half. Apply glue to the back center of the waist and attach the folded ends of the ribbons.

7. Bring both ribbons around to the angel's front. Tie a 1½-inch bow at the front center of the waist.

ANGEL'S WINGS:

1. To make the wings, fold the 12-inch length of pattern paper in half, bringing the 3½-inch sides together. Open up. Run a thin line of glue down the center line.

2. Fold in the right half, placing the 3½-inch end on the glue line. Run another thin line of glue down the center line. Fold in the left half, placing the 3½-inch end on the glue line.

3. Gather the paper together at the center line, forming wings.

4. Apply glue to the back center of the blouse and attach the wings.

FINISHING:

1. Place the third 18-inch length of off-white ribbon on top of the 18-inch-length of pale blue ribbon. Make a 1-inch-diameter loopy bow. Tie off the bow with the 6-inch length of ribbon. (See Introduction, page 5, for instructions on making a loopy bow.)

2. Glue bow to the top of the hair.

3. Fold the 8-inch length of ribbon in half. Glue the open end to the base of the bow.

Beaded Wreath

1. Glue one end of both bead strings to the rear of the wreath.

2. Wrap both strings of beads around the wreath. Finish by gluing the ends of both strings to the rear of the wreath where the strings were first glued.

3. Clip the stems from the roses and leaves. Glue them to the front of the wreath between two rows of beads.

4. Place the 18-inch length of blue ribbon on top of the two lengths of mauve ribbon. Make a 2-inch bow. Glue the bow to the top of the wreath. (The roses and leaves should be positioned at the lower right of the wreath.)

5. Fold the 12-inch length of blue ribbon in half and tie an overhand knot near the open end. Glue the folded end just behind the bow.

What You'll Need

3-inch bleached grapevine wreath
22-inch string mauve 3-mm beads
22-inch string blue 3-mm beads
Hot glue mini gun
Wire cutters
3 blue ribbon roses, ¼ inch each
2 rose leaves, ½ inch each
18 inches blue ⅛-inch ribbon
2 lengths mauve ¹⁄₁₆-inch ribbon,
18 inches each
12 inches blue ⅛-inch ribbon

O CHRISTMAS TREE!

WHAT YOU'LL NEED

2 swatches green pattern material,
6-inch squares
Pen or pencil
Scissors
6-inch square polyester batting
Sewing machine
Thread to match the green material
1 yard of mini-garland
Needle
4 wooden mini-ornaments
4 gold mini-ornaments, 8 mm each
3 gold mini-ornaments, 6 mm each
White craft glue
11 red bows, 3/8 inch each
(or 18 inches of red 1/16-inch ribbon
to make bows)
9 inches red 1/16-inch ribbon
12 inches red 1/4-inch ribbon

1. Cut out the pattern for "O Christmas Tree!" See page 64 for the pattern. See Introduction, page 5, for instructions on cutting out patterns.

2. Place the pattern on the wrong side of the green material. Trace the pattern on the material; cut out the tree figure, allowing a 1/4-inch seam allowance. Repeat once with the green material and once with one thickness of batting.

3. Place the right sides of the two tree figures together. Place the batting on top of the green material.

4. Sew the batting and the two tree figures together, leaving an opening at the base of the tree. Sew again, to reinforce the seams.

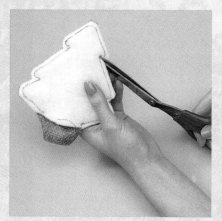

5. Trim the seams and clip the curves of the tree.

6. Turn the tree right side out. Baste the opening shut.

7. Attach the garland to the tree by spot basting on the seams. (If you have garland left over, apply a spot of glue to the knot at the end of the nylon line and attach to the tree.)

8. Baste the ornaments onto the tree in a random pattern.

9. Cover the basting by gluing 1/2-inch bows over the knots.

10. Fold the 9-inch length of red ribbon in half. Glue the open end to the tree top.

11. Make a 1 1/4-inch bow from the 12-inch length of red ribbon. Glue over the glued end of the ribbon in step 10.

Buttons are hot and this Santa has plenty of them. Hang Button-Down Santa on your tree or on a doorknob, or sit him on the mantle to greet your children on Christmas morning.

WHAT YOU'LL NEED

Scissors
12-inch-square swatch red felt
Matching red thread for sewing machine
12-inch-square swatch black felt
Matching black thread for sewing machine
12-inch-square swatch muslin
Matching off-white thread for sewing machine
12-inch-square swatch burlap
Matching beige thread for sewing machine
Pins
Sewing machine
Polyester fiberfill
Needle
2 spools extra-strong cream-color thread; we used Coats Dual Duty Extra Strong #116
1 spool black thread; we used Coats Dual Duty Extra Strong, Black
70 or more buttons; two holes, various colors (white, off-white, black, and red), and various sizes (mostly $3/8$ inch, some $3/4$ inch)
Permanent black marker
15 inches jute twine, for sack
Permanent red marker
Pencil
Red embroidery thread (321 DMC)
Blue embroidery thread (312 DMC)
White craft glue
2 lengths jute twine, for legs, 7 inches each
24 inches jute twine, for hanger and bow

1. Cut out all patterns. See pages 62–63 for the "Button-Down Santa" patterns. See Introduction, page 5, for directions on cutting out patterns. Allow a ¼-inch seam allowance for sewing.

2. Place the suit and hat patterns on the red felt and cut 2 Santa's suits, 2 hats, and 2 hatbands. Place the boot pattern on the black felt and cut 4 boots. Place the body pattern on the muslin and cut 2 bodies. Cut an 8-inch by 3½-inch piece from the burlap.

SANTA'S SUIT:

1. Fold both pieces of red felt along the fold lines (indicated on the pattern) at the lower edge. Pin in place.

2. Using the matching red thread, sew along sew line A (indicated on the pattern) for all four corners.

3. With the right sides of the red felt pieces together, sew the front and back together along sew line B, leaving the sleeves and neck open. (See the pattern for location of sewing lines.)

4. Clip the corners. Turn the suit right side out. Stuff the suit three-quarters full with polyester fiberfill.

SANTA'S BODY:
1. Place the right sides of the 2 pieces of muslin together. Using matching thread, sew along the sew lines (indicated on the pattern), leaving the bottom edge open.

2. Clip the curves. Turn the body right side out. Stuff the body with polyester fiberfill. Baste the lower edge shut.

3. Compress and slide the bottom of Santa's body into the suit through the neck.

4. Thread the needle with about 20 inches extra-strong cream-color thread, doubled. Tie an overhand knot about 2 inches from the ends.

5. Take a running stitch about 3/16 inch from the edge of the neck on Santa's suit. Pull the thread to gather the suit's neck close to the body's neck. Tie off the thread and trim any excess.

SANTA'S HAT:
1. Sew (using matching red thread) one of Santa's hatbands to the lower edge of Santa's hat, wrong sides together. Do the same for the other hatband and hat.

2. Put the 2 hats on top of each other, wrong sides together. Sew (using matching red thread) only the hatband edges together.

3. Turn the hat so the right sides are together and sew (using matching red thread) the rest of the hat together.

4. Turn the hat right side out. Turn the hatband up 3/4 inch. The seam connecting the hatband to the hat should not show.

5. Thread the needle with extra-strong cream-color thread, doubled. Tie a knot 1/4 inch from the ends. Insert the needle along the hatband and pull through about 1/4 inch away from the original insertion. Tie a knot next to the hatband and clip the thread to 1/4 inch. Repeat until hatband is filled with many knots. The knot arrangement is random and occasionally interspersed with the extra-strong black thread and knots.

BUTTON-DOWN SANTA

6. To make the tassel, thread needle with extra-strong cream-color thread, doubled. Draw the needle through the hat's peak. Leave about 1½ inches of thread hanging free on either side of the peak. Repeat until tassel is full.

SANTA'S BOOTS:

1. Place the boots with the right sides together. Using matching black thread, sew the boots together along the sew line (indicated in the pattern). Leave the tops of the boots open.

2. Clip the curves. Turn the boots right side out. Stuff each boot with polyester fiberfill.

3. Thread the needle with about 20 inches extra-strong black thread, doubled. Make an overhand knot about 2 inches from the ends. Take a running stitch about ³/₁₆ inch from the upper edge of the boot. Pull the thread to gather the top of the boot shut. Tie off the thread and trim any excess.

SANTA'S LEGS:

1. Thread the needle with about 20 inches extra-strong cream-color thread, doubled. Tie an overhand knot near the ends; clip excess thread to ¹/₈ inch.

2. Insert the needle into the side of a boot and up through the center of the gathering. Begin threading buttons for the legs. Start with a ³/₄-inch button to cover the top of the boot. Place a ³/₄-inch red button about 1¼ inches up the stack.

3. When the stack of buttons reaches about 2½ inches, insert the needle into Santa's bottom about ½ inch in from Santa's side. Bring the needle back out of Santa's bottom about ¼ inch away.

4. Take the thread back down the stack of buttons, through the second hole in each button. Insert the needle down through the center of the boot's gathering and out the side of the boot, just below gathering stitch. Allow a little room on the thread to add a jute twine bow later. Knot the thread and clip any excess. Use the black marker to color any thread that shows around the top of the boot.

5. Repeat for Santa's other leg.

SANTA'S SACK:

1. Fold the burlap in half, bringing the 3½-inch sides together.

2. Using the matching thread, sew the sides together, leaving the top of the sack open.

3. Turn the sack inside out and stuff about three-quarters full with polyester fiberfill.

4. Gather the top of the sack about 1 inch from the opening. Wrap the 15-inch length of twine around the gathering and tie a 2³/₄-inch bow.

SANTA'S ARMS:

1. Thread the needle with about 20 inches of extra-strong cream-color thread, doubled. Tie a knot near the ends and clip excess thread to ¹/₈ inch.

2. Insert the needle into the cuff of Santa's suit about ³/₁₆ inch from the edge. Take a running stitch around the cuff. Pull the thread to gather the cuff. Tie off the thread, but do not cut it.

3. Begin threading buttons for the arms. Start with a ³/₄-inch white button; follow with a ³/₄-inch red button.

4. When about 1 inch of buttons have been threaded, insert the needle through the gathered area of Santa's sack and out the other side. String buttons in reverse order for Santa's other arm.

5. Insert the needle into the second cuff about ³/₁₆ inch from the edge. Take a running stitch around the cuff. Pull the thread to gather the cuff. Tie off the thread, but do not cut it.

6. Insert the needle back through the second hole in each button, through the sack, and through the second group of buttons.

7. Insert the needle through the gathered material at the cuff and out below the gathering stitches. Knot the thread and clip off any excess. Use the red marker to color any thread that shows around the gathering at the cuffs.

SANTA'S FACE:
1. With the pencil, draw Santa's lower lip and mark the eye placement (indicated on the pattern).

2. Use the red embroidery thread to satin stitch Santa's lower lip. Use the blue embroidery thread to stitch French knots for Santa's eyes.

3. To make Santa's hair, moustache, and beard, thread the needle with extra-strong cream-color thread. Insert the needle into Santa's head and take a ¼-inch stitch, leaving about 2 inches hanging free on either side of the stitch. (Do not tie any knots.)

4. Repeat until the hair and beard are thick. When finished, trim the thread to shape the hair and beard. For the moustache, trim the hanging ends to ½ inch.

FINISHING:
1. Apply white craft glue to the inside rim of Santa's hat. Place the hat on Santa's head with the seams to each side. Hold until the glue sets.

2. To make the leg bows, wrap the 7-inch lengths of jute twine around the legs just above the ¾-inch button next to the boots. Tie a 1½-inch bow.

3. Fold the 24-inch length of jute twine in half. Knot the twine around the base of the tassel about 5 inches down from the folded end. Tie a 2-inch bow with the remaining twine. Trim the ends to 2 inches.

4. Apply a dab of white glue to the back of the twine and tassel so the knot won't slip off. Let dry.

TIPS AND VARIATIONS
If you fill Santa's bottom with dried beans, he will sit on your mantle.

TEXAS THEME TREE

❧

Put a new and
different spin on your
Christmas celebration
by selecting a
Texas theme for
your tree. Decorate
your tree with unique
ornaments that say
Lone Star State:
bandannas, cowboys,
longhorn steers,
and more. You can
complete your Texas tree
with pointers on garlands,
toppers, and skirts from
the Introduction.

SHERIFF

HOLLY BADGE

WHAT YOU'LL NEED

½-inch brush
2-inch 5-pointed wooden star
Acrylic paints: yellow and black
5/0 red sable brush
Wire cutters
2 holly leaves, ½-inch leaves
⅛-inch stamen
Hot glue mini gun
2 inches red ⅛-inch ribbon
8 inches gold elastic cord

1. Using the ½-inch brush, paint both sides of the star yellow.

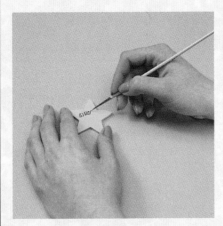

2. Using the 5/0 red sable brush, paint "Sheriff" in black.

3. Trim the stems from the holly leaves and the stamen. Glue the leaves and stamen on the star at the lower right of the star.

4. Make a ¾-inch bow from the ribbon. Glue the bow just above the holly leaves.

5. Fold the gold cord in half. Tie an overhand knot near the open end. Glue the knot to the rear of the star's top point.

TIPS AND VARIATIONS

You don't have to use a 5-pointed star; in the old West, sheriff badges came in many shapes and sizes. There were also U.S. Marshals and Texas Rangers in the old West; make an entire collection!

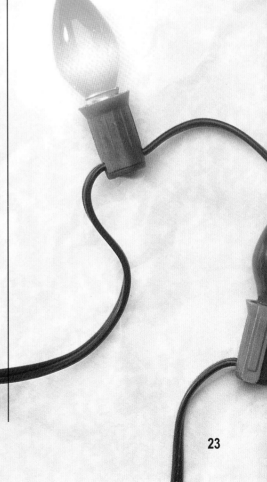

1. Cut out all patterns. See page 61 for the "Texas Santa" patterns. See Introduction, page 5, for directions on cutting out patterns.

2. Place the patterns on the felt: red for the main figure and lips; white for the chaps, cuffs, beard, hatband, and hat pom-pom; black for the belt; and gold for the belt buckle. Trace the patterns onto the felt with a pen or pencil (use chalk for the black felt).

4. Glue the following pieces in place using white craft glue: hat pom-pom, hatband, beard, lips, belt, belt buckle, chaps, and cuffs. Let dry.

What You'll Need

Scissors
Felt squares: red, white, black, and gold
Pen or pencil
Chalk
White craft glue
Polyester craft batting
Wire cutters
2 holly leaves, ½-inch leaves
Hot glue mini gun
⅛-inch stamen
10 inches gold thread
Needle

3. Following the lines traced on the red felt, cut out the main figure. The side showing the lines will be called the wrong side. Cut out the lips from the red felt. Following the lines traced on the white, black, and gold felt squares, cut out the chaps, cuffs, beard, hatband, hat pom-pom, belt, and belt buckle.

5. Place the pattern of the main figure on the black felt. Outline the general shape using chalk. Allow at least ½ inch outside the main figure (don't forget to include room for the chaps).

6. Cut out the general shape from the black felt.

7. Place the pattern of the main figure on one thickness of batting. Trace the general shape with a pen or pencil.

8. Move ¼ inch inside the tracing and cut out the figure.

9. On the wrong side of the figure, run a thin line of white craft glue around the edge.

10. Place the batting on top of the wrong side of the figure and inside the line of glue.

11. Pick up the figure and batting; be sure not to touch the glue or let the batting slip.

12. Place the figure and batting on top of the black felt from step 6. Press the edges of the figure onto the black felt. Continue pressing until the glue sets and the figure sticks to the black felt. Set aside until glue dries (about 20 minutes).

13. Trim the black felt to within ⅛ inch of the figure.

14. Trim the stems from the holly leaves and glue to the hat using hot glue.

15. Glue the stamen on the holly leaves using hot glue.

16. Double thread the needle with gold thread. Draw the needle through the pom-pom.

17. Tie an overhand knot about 4 inches above the figure. Cut off any excess thread.

TIPS AND VARIATIONS

Try tracing the pattern on ¼-inch-thick basswood, available at hobby shops. Then use a scroll saw to cut out the ornament. Paint the wood in your favorite colors with acrylic paints.

Instead of glue, sew the figure to the black felt backing using a fancy stitch in a contrasting color thread.

1. Cover the entire horse with two coats of white paint.

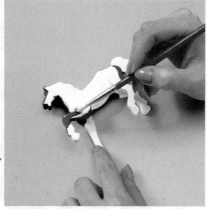

2. Apply brown pinto markings.

3. Slip the 8-inch length of ribbon through the wreath and tie an overhand knot about ½ inch from the open end. Reshape the wreath from a circle into an oval.

6. Using the tweezers, glue the jingle bells evenly around the wreath.

WHAT YOU'LL NEED

Carved horse, 4 inches by 3½ inches
½-inch brush
Acrylic paints: white and brown
8 inches red ⅛-inch ribbon
2-inch frosted sisal wreath
White craft glue
5 inches red ⅛-inch ribbon
Tweezers
7 jingle bells, 6 mm each

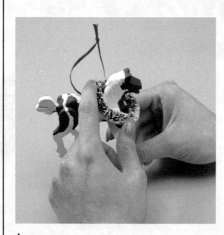

4. Apply glue at the bottom of the horse's mane. Slip the wreath over the horse's head, placing the ribbon in the glue. Hold the wreath and ribbon in place until the glue sets.

5. Make a ¾-inch bow with the 5-inch length of ribbon. Glue to the wreath on the right front side.

TIPS AND VARIATIONS

Paint the horse to match your favorite breed; an encyclopedia will have photographs of many breeds of horses. Painting the horse turquoise and pink will give you a horse with a Southwestern style.

Pepper Yule Party

What You'll Need

12 plastic red peppers, ⁷/₈ inch each
18 inches red ¹/₈-inch ribbon
18 inches green ¹/₈-inch ribbon
Hot glue mini gun
8 inches red ¹/₈-inch ribbon
8 inches green ¹/₈-inch ribbon

1. Braid three peppers together.

2. In the second row, add a pepper each time you twist one of the three braiding wires from the first row (French braid). Continue adding peppers.

3. After all 12 peppers have been braided in, continue braiding the wires together.

4. Bend the braided wire behind the peppers to form a hook.

5. Using the 18-inch lengths of red and green ribbon, make a 3-inch bow. Glue the bow to the top of the peppers.

6. Insert the red and green 8-inch lengths of ribbon through the braided wire hook. Tie an overhand knot 1 inch from the open ends.

Tips and Variations

You can make a nice arrangement for your front door by using much larger red peppers.

In many European countries, it is traditional to hang fruit and sometimes vegetables on a Christmas tree. You can create a similar effect using miniature fruits and vegetables. Just be sure there are wires to braid.

If the red coating on the peppers chips, red fingernail polish works as a great touch-up.

CHRISTMAS KERCHIEF

Iron
1 standard 18-inch-square red bandanna
2 glazed 3-leaved holly picks, ¾-inch leaves
Hot glue mini gun
8 gold-brushed alder cones
8 inches red ⅛-inch ribbon
Red thread
Needle

1. Iron the bandanna flat. Fold and iron the plain border underneath so that only the design area shows.

2. Fold the bandanna into a triangular shape. Iron flat again.

3. Fold the long edge up ½ inch. Continue folding in same direction until about 2 inches remain unfolded at the tip of the bandanna.

4. The tip should be at the center of the folded bandanna. Fold the bandanna in half, using the tip as the center. Tie a square knot about 4 inches from the center tip.

5. Pull the ends of the bandanna out from the square knot. Iron the ends flat.

6. Insert a holly pick into each side of the knot. Shoot a little hot glue into each side to hold the holly in place.

7. Arrange the alder cones into two groups of four. Apply hot glue to the stems of one group and place it in on one side of the knot. Repeat for the other side.

8. Fold the ribbon in half and tie an overhand knot near the open end. Sew the folded end to the back of the square knot.

TIPS AND VARIATIONS

Bandannas come in many colors. A turquoise or pink bandanna provides a Southwestern-style ornament.

1. Fold the 20-inch length of leather in half. Make sure colored sides of the leather are up and flat.

2. Starting at the top rear of the bolo, thread at least 3½ inches of the open end through the openings in the bolo.

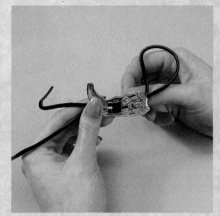

3. Again starting at the top rear of the bolo, thread the 1-inch length of leather into the bolo openings between the strands of the 20-inch piece. Trim any excess at the top or bottom of the bolo.

WHAT YOU'LL NEED

20 inches ⅛-inch-wide leather
2-inch bolo
1 inch ⅛-inch-wide leather

TIPS AND VARIATIONS

Bolos come in many different metals and shapes. When choosing additional shapes, be sure the leather will feed through the bolo's holes.

COWGIRL HAT

1. Fold the tricolor cord in half. Glue the halfway point to the side of the hat crown.

2. Loosely cross the cord on the other side of the crown and glue in place.

3. Trim the ends of the cord so they overhang the hat brim by ⅛ inch. Glue the ends to the hat brim.

4. Push the points of a rhinestone setting through the hat brim from underneath to the top. Place a rhinestone into the points.

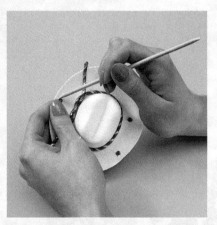

5. Using the orange stick, push the points over the rhinestone to hold it in place. Repeat until all rhinestones have been placed around the brim, alternating red and green rhinestones.

6. Fold the elastic cord in half and tie an overhand knot about an inch from the open end. Glue the knot to the bottom front edge of the brim.

WHAT YOU'LL NEED

12 inches tricolor 4-mm cord
4-inch white Stetson
Hot glue mini gun
14 rhinestone settings, 4-mm size
7 green rhinestones, 4 mm each
7 red rhinestones, 4 mm each
Orange stick
8 inches gold elastic cord

TIPS AND VARIATIONS

For variety, use miniature felt cowboy/cowgirl hats in different colors or shapes. You can also vary the look by choosing studs other than rhinestones. Instead of tricolor cord, glue lace around the brim for a more feminine look.

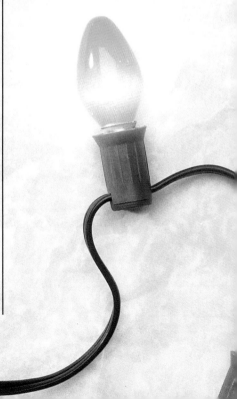

Red-Hot Wreath

1. Make a ⅞-inch bow from the 3-inch length of ribbon.

2. Trim the stems from the red peppers. Glue in place on the wreath.

3. Glue the bow in place just above the peppers.

4. Insert the 10-inch length of ribbon through the center of the wreath. Match the ends of the ribbon, then put a dab of glue on the top rear of the wreath to fix the ribbon in place. Tie an overhand knot 3 inches above the wreath. Make a 1½-inch bow above the overhand knot.

JOLLY CLAY SANTA

WHAT YOU'LL NEED

#02 FIMO, face color
Toothpicks
Paring knife
Wire cutters
Paper clip
Rolling pin
#29 FIMO, red
#0 FIMO, white
5/0 red sable brush
Acrylic paints: white and blue
Baking sheet
½-inch brush
FIMO water-based gloss varnish
8 inches white ⅛-inch ribbon

1. Start Santa's head with a basic 2-inch egg shape in #02 FIMO. Add small balls and "snakes" to build up the forehead, nose, cheeks, and eyes. Use toothpicks as well as your fingers to place the balls and snakes; use the paring knife to refine Santa's face.

2. Snip off the small end of a paper clip. Push about half of the remaining "U" shape into the top of Santa's head, open end facing down.

3. Using the rolling pin, roll a snake ⅛-inch diameter by ⅜-inch length from the #29 FIMO. Shape into an arc and place about ¼ inch below Santa's nose. This will be Santa's lower lip.

4. Roll about 25 snakes, ⅛-inch diameter, from #0 FIMO. Press one end of each snake onto the face and drape gracefully to form the beard. Taper the beard ends with your fingertips.

5. Roll four snakes from the #0 FIMO. The snakes should be about ¾ inch long, starting with a diameter of ⅛ inch and tapering to a point. Press two onto the face above the lips for Santa's mustache; press two above the eyes for Santa's eyebrows.

6. Using the rolling pin, roll out a shape from the #29 FIMO that is about 2½ inches by 4 inches and ⅛ inch thick. Use the paring knife to cut a triangle with a 2½-inch base. This will be Santa's hat.

7. Drape and press the base of the triangle across Santa's forehead. Pull the tip of the triangle down to the side of the base.

8. Make about 34 balls of several different sizes from #0 FIMO. Press them in a random arrangement along the bottom ½ inch of the hat's base. These will form the white cuff of Santa's hat.

9. Make several more balls from #0 FIMO. Press these on the tip of Santa's hat.

10. Paint Santa's eyes white using the 5/0 brush and the white acrylic paint. Let dry. Mix a small amount of the white and blue acrylic paints together to create a light blue color. Paint the iris of Santa's eyes light blue. Let dry. Paint Santa's pupils dark blue, using only the blue acrylic paint.

11. Move the ornament to a baking sheet. (You may want to use a spatula to move the ornament.) Bake at 200 degrees Fahrenheit for 2 hours. Let cool.

12. Using the ½-inch brush, paint the ornament with FIMO water-based gloss varnish. Let dry 24 hours.

13. Thread the 8-inch length of white ribbon through the paper clip. Tie an overhand knot near the open end.

TIPS AND VARIATIONS

You can make many Christmas ornaments from FIMO clay; let your imagination run wild.

A low temperature and long baking time were used because Santa's head has a lot of white color and the egg shape is so thick. Don't hurry the baking process by turning the oven to a high temperature; this will cause scorching and burning. Generally, the longer the FIMO clay is baked, the stronger it will be.

2 lengths iridescent 3½-inch-wide paper twist, 5 inches each

Hot glue mini gun

5-inch gold grape spray

⅝-inch diameter wooden angel head (with drilled hole)

Wood wool

3 holly leaves, 1½ inches each

Wire cutters

18 inches white, gold edged ½-inch ribbon

8 inches white ⅛-inch ribbon

1. Untwist and open the paper twist. Fold each in half, bringing the 3½-inch sides together.

2. Gather the open ends together. Glue the gathered ends. These will be the angel's wings.

3. Glue the gathered ends of the wings to the backside of the grape spray stem.

4. Slip the head down the grape stem until it sits on top of the wings. Glue the head in place.

5. Compress about a 1-inch-diameter clump of wood wool. Apply glue to the hair area of the angel's head. Arrange wood wool on top of the angel's head around the stem.

6. Bend the grape spray stem back to touch the back of the angel's head.

7. Clip the stems from the holly leaves. Glue the leaves under angel's chin.

8. Make a 3-inch bow from the 18-inch length of ribbon. Glue the bow under the angel's chin on top of the holly leaves.

9. Slip one end of the 8-inch length of ribbon through the loop made from the stem. Fold the ribbon in half and tie an overhand knot ½ inch from the open end.

DOVE OF PEACE

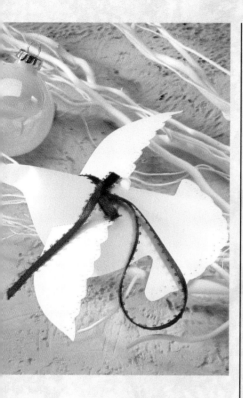

WHAT YOU'LL NEED

1 sheet 80-pound drawing paper
Pencil
Scissors
Craft knife
Pin
Rubber cement
8 inches burgundy ¼-inch
looped ribbon
Hot glue mini gun
12 inches burgundy ¼-inch
looped ribbon

1. Cut out all patterns. See page 63 for the "Dove of Peace" patterns. See Introduction, page 5, for directions on cutting out patterns.

2. Trace the patterns on drawing paper.

3. Cut out the bird and wings with scissors and craft knife.

4. Slice slits for the wings (indicated on the pattern).

5. On the backside of the paper, draw a line about ⅛ inch in from the edge that follows the outline of the wings and tail.

6. Following the lines, poke a pinhole through the paper every ⅛ inch.

7. Fold ½ inch of the bird's head together, matching the beaks. Bond the head together using rubber cement.

8. Poke a pinhole through the paper at the eye mark (indicated on the pattern).

9. Slide the wings through the slits and center.

10. Fold the 8-inch length of ribbon in half. Glue the open end to the bird's body above the shoulders (indicated on the pattern).

11. Make a 1-inch bow from the 12-inch length of ribbon.

12. Glue the bow over the ends of the 8-inch length of ribbon.

CHILDREN'S THEME TREE

Your young ones will
absolutely love
the clever ornaments
you make to decorate
a theme tree
just for children.
Dinosaurs, teddy bears,
and snowmen
will prance about
your tree on
Christmas morning. Be
sure to see the
Introduction for
some great suggestions
for Children's tree skirts,
garlands, and toppers.

POM-POM SNOWMAN

WHAT YOU'LL NEED

2½-inch pom-pom

2-inch pom-pom

1-inch pom-pom

Hot glue mini gun

⅝-inch top hat

3½-inch broom

8-inch striped knit scarf,
⅞ inch wide

½-inch plastic carrot

Wire cutters

2 goggle eyes, 4 mm each

3 black buttons, 4 mm each

White craft glue

Tweezers

8 inches white ⅛-inch ribbon

1. Pushing acrylic puff aside, find the center of the 2½-inch and 2-inch pom-poms. Glue centers together with hot glue. Attach the 1-inch pom-pom to the 2-inch pom-pom in the same manner and in line with the 2½-inch pom-pom, forming a "snowman."

2. Apply hot glue to the underside of the top hat; attach to the top of the 1-inch pom-pom.

3. Lay the broom diagonally across the snowman with the upper end touching the underside of the hat's brim. Hot glue the upper end of the broom to the underside of the hat's brim. Let dry.

4. Using hot glue, attach the lower part of the broom to the bottom pom-pom.

5. Fold the striped scarf in half lengthwise. Insert the scarf through the space between the head and the broom. Knot the scarf at the side of the head. Unfold scarf ends.

6. Snip off the carrot top. Apply hot glue to the carrot's end and place for the snowman's nose.

7. Using white glue and tweezers, place the snowman's eyes and buttons.

8. Fold the ribbon in half; make an overhand knot ½ inch from the open end. Using hot glue, attach the folded half to the center top of the top hat.

DINOSAUR IN DECEMBER

WHAT YOU'LL NEED

Scissors

Felt squares: bright blue and
bright yellow

Pen or pencil

Polyester craft batting

White craft glue

6-mm goggle eye

10 inches gold thread

Needle

1. Cut out all patterns. See page 61 for the "Dinosaur in December" patterns. See Introduction, page 5, for directions on cutting out patterns.

2. Place the pattern for the main figure on the blue felt square. Trace the pattern with a pen or pencil.

3. Following the traced lines, cut out the figure. The side with the tracing lines will be called the wrong side.

4. Place the pattern for the main figure on the bright yellow felt.

5. Trace the general shape of the figure at least ½ inch beyond the figure.

6. Following the traced lines, cut out the general shape. This will serve as the backing.

7. Unfold one thickness of batting. Trace the pattern of the main figure on the batting.

8. Move ¼ inch inside the traced pattern and redraw the pattern.

9. Cut out the figure, following the inner traced line.

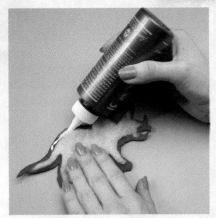

10. Place the batting on top of the wrong side of the blue felt. (There should be about a ¼-inch space between the edge of the batting and the edge of the figure.) Run a thin line of craft glue at the edge of the figure.

11. Pick up the figure and batting; be sure not to touch the glue or let the batting slip. Place the figure and batting on top of the backing material (the yellow felt). Press the edges of the figure onto the backing until the glue sets and the figure sticks to the backing. Set aside until the glue dries (about 20 minutes).

12. Trim the backing material to within ⅛ inch of the figure. However, leave extra backing along the spine; slightly scallop this section.

13. Cut out different-size triangular shapes from the yellow felt. These will serve as trim.

14. Fold the triangles in half and cut a nip out of the bottom of the triangles. Open flat.

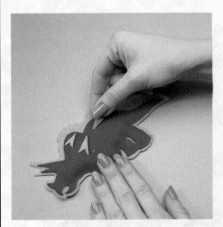

15. In a random arrangement, glue the triangles to the dinosaur's front.

16. Glue the goggle eye in place for the dinosaur's eye.

17. Thread the needle with the gold thread.

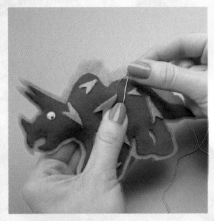

18. Draw the needle through the dinosaur's spine (through both pieces of felt) in the middle.

19. Tie an overhand knot about 4 inches above the figure. Cut off any excess thread.

TIPS AND VARIATIONS

Trace the pattern on a ¼-inch-thick piece of basswood; use a scroll saw to cut out the figure. Decorate with acrylic paints.

Instead of glue, use a fancy stitch in a contrasting color to sew the figure to the backing.

BEARS ON A SLEIGH RIDE

WHAT YOU'LL NEED

4½-inch sleigh
½-inch brush
Red enamel paint
Red oak stain
Assorted bears:
2 pandas, 1½ inches each
1¼-inch koala
2 sitting whites, 1 inch each
1-inch sitting dark brown
1¾-inch standing teddy
1½-inch sitting teddy
3 dark browns, ¾ inch each
Hot glue mini gun
5 candy canes, ⅝ inch each
10 inches tricolor 4-mm cord
5 inches tricolor 4-mm cord
Wire cutters
2 holly leaves, ½-inch leaves
⅛-inch stamen
2 inches red ⅛-inch ribbon
1-inch sisal wreath
White craft glue
Frosted glitter

1. Paint the carriage section (inside, outside, and underneath) of the sleigh red.

2. Stain the runners.

3. Starting at the left rear of the sleigh, hot glue the bears in place in the following counterclockwise order: standing teddy*, koala*, panda, sitting teddy*, sitting dark brown, panda*, and sitting white*. Be sure to vary the direction the bears face. Glue the other sitting white* in the center of the sleigh facing front.

4. Glue the three smaller dark brown bears wherever there is a hole in the bear arrangement.

5. Using hot glue, attach a candy cane to the left paw of all asterisked (*) bears.

6. Sear the ends of the tricolor cords to prevent unraveling.

7. Using hot glue, attach one end of the 10-inch length of tricolor cord to the sleigh's front; attach the other end to the sleigh's rear.

8. Make a 2-inch bow from the 5-inch length of cord. Using hot glue, attach the bow to the sleigh's front to cover the end of the 10-inch length of cord.

9. Trim the stems from the holly leaves. Attach above the bow, using hot glue. Trim the stem from the stamen and attach where holly leaves touch, using hot glue.

10. Make a 1-inch bow from the 2-inch length of red ⅛-inch ribbon. Some sisal wreaths come with a felt bow. If your wreath has a bow, remove it. In its place, attach the 1-inch bow using hot glue.

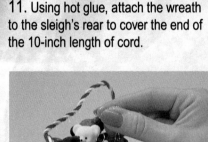

11. Using hot glue, attach the wreath to the sleigh's rear to cover the end of the 10-inch length of cord.

12. Spread white glue over the tops of runners, the top edge of the sleigh, the tops of the bears' heads, and the top of the wreath. Sprinkle on frosted glitter.

TIPS AND VARIATIONS

Craft stores generally carry a wide assortment of animals. Fill the sleigh with your personal favorites.

If you cannot find tiny dark brown bears, use ½-inch prewrapped packages.

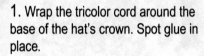

WHAT YOU'LL NEED

4-inch sombrero
8 inches tricolor 3-mm cord
Hot glue mini gun
Wire cutters
¾-inch glazed holly leaf pick
2 red stamens, ⅛ inch each
6-mm jingle bell
3 plaid stockings, 1½ inches each
3 Santa hats, ¾ inch each
8 inches gold elastic cord

1. Wrap the tricolor cord around the base of the hat's crown. Spot glue in place.

2. Trim the ends of the cord at an angle. Apply a dab of glue to each end to prevent unraveling. Glue the ends to the edge of the brim.

3. Take apart the holly pick and trim the stems from the leaves. Glue in place where the cord overlaps at the crown's base.

4. Glue the stamens onto each holly leaf. Glue the bell where cord overlaps at the crown's base.

5. Turn the hat over. Glue the Santa hats and plaid stockings at the edge of the hat's brim. The hats and stockings should alternate and be evenly spaced.

6. Turn hat upright. Fold the gold cord in half. Tie an overhand knot ½ inch from the open end. Glue the folded end to the top center of the crown.

NOEL ROCKING HORSE

3-inch embroidery frame
Walnut stain
½-inch brush
5-inch-square muslin
Scissors
Hot glue mini gun
10 inches green ½-inch eyelet
5 inches red ¼-inch looped ribbon
8 inches red ¼-inch looped ribbon
3-inch rocking horse
Acrylic paints: white, red, green, and yellow
5/0 red sable brush

1. Using ½-inch brush, stain embroidery frame.

2. Stretch the muslin in the frame. Trim any excess material.

3. Glue eyelet to the back of the frame; overlap the eyelet's ends.

4. Make a 1-inch bow from the 5-inch length of ribbon. Glue to the top of the frame to cover the space in the outer frame.

5. Insert the 8-inch length of ribbon through the gap in the frame hardware. Tie an overhand knot ½ inch from the open end.

6. Paint the horse's mane white. Let dry. Paint the horse's body red. Let dry. If necessary, give a second coat.

7. Paint the rocker green. Let dry. Paint the saddle green. Let dry. If necessary, give a second coat. (The horse's ears and the tips of the rocker will overhang the frame. Be sure to paint the back of the figure in these areas. Also remember to paint the edges of the horse.)

8. Paint the mane yellow. Let dry. If necessary, give a second coat.

9. Using the 5/0 brush, add yellow trim to the rocker and saddle areas. Add a green bow and braid to the mane and an eyelid and eyelashes.

10. Glue horse to muslin.

WHAT YOU'LL NEED

2-inch partridge
Wire cutters
2½-inch bark nest
Hot glue mini gun
8 inches red ⅛-inch ribbon
Moss
24 inches red ¼-inch looped ribbon
6 inches red ¼-inch looped ribbon

1. Snip the wire from the bird's feet.

2. Glue the bird into the nest's opening.

3. Thread the 8-inch length of ribbon through the hook at the top of the nest. Tie an overhand knot ½ inch from the ends.

4. Arrange and glue the moss around the hook and ribbon.

5. Make a 2½-inch loopy bow from the 24-inch length of ribbon. Tie off the bow with the 6-inch length of ribbon.

6. Glue the loopy bow to the moss in front of the hook and ribbon.

TIPS AND VARIATIONS

Instead of moss, sprinkle on crystal glitter to make it look like a snow-covered nest.

Try a different type of bird: cardinal, blue jay, robin, or any other bird that strikes your fancy.

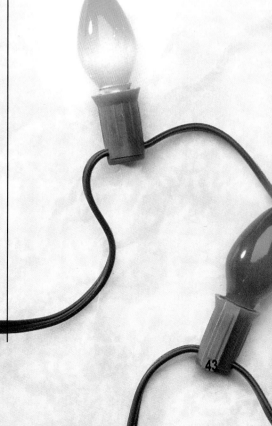

1. Glue the ³⁄₄-inch packages into the sleigh, starting at the right front corner. About ¼ inch to ½ inch of the packages should show above the side of the sleigh.

2. Glue the ½-inch packages into the sleigh, starting at the left front corner. The bottom of the first ½-inch package should sit on the front corner of sleigh.

3. Make a ³⁄₄-inch bow from the 3-inch length of red ribbon.

4. Remove the bow that came on the wreath. Glue the ³⁄₄-inch bow in its place. Set the wreath aside.

5. Glue the candy canes into the left rear corner of the sleigh.

6. Glue the wreath in front of the candy canes.

7. Glue one end of the 8-inch length of gold cord to the front of the sleigh; glue the other end to the rear of the sleigh.

8. Make two 1-inch bows from the 4-inch lengths of gold cord. Glue one bow at each end of the 8-inch length of gold cord.

WHAT YOU'LL NEED

4-inch wicker sleigh
Hot glue mini gun
3 gift packages, ³⁄₄ inch each
2 gift packages, ½ inch each
3 inches red ⅛-inch ribbon
1½-inch sisal wreath
2 candy canes, 2³⁄₄ inches each
8 inches gold elastic cord
2 lengths gold elastic cord,
4 inches each

TIPS AND VARIATIONS

Instead of gift packages, fill the sleigh with candy, bears, small flowers, miniature sports equipment, or a special gift such as an engagement ring.

BRAIDED CANDY CANE

4. Place 1 length of red ribbon on top of 1 length of white ribbon. Fold in half and glue the ends together. Glue the ends to the top edge of the candy cane.

5. Place the second length of red ribbon on top of the second length of white ribbon. Make a 1½-inch bow and glue over the ends of the other ribbons.

1. Turn up the long edge of one of the strips of calico ¼ inch. Iron flat. Enclose a length of florist wire into the fold. Continue making ¼-inch folds until you have a strip ¼ inch wide by 13 inches long. Clip florist wire that sticks out from the strip. Repeat with the other two strips of material.

2. Braid the three strips together.

WHAT YOU'LL NEED

2 strips red calico, 1½ inches by 13 inches each

1½-inch by 13-inch white with red dots strip of material

Iron

3 lengths covered florist wire, 18 inches each

Wire cutters

Hot glue mini gun

Scissors

2 lengths red ⅛-inch ribbon, 8 inches each

2 lengths white ⅛-inch ribbon, 8 inches each

3. Turn the ends back on themselves and glue in place. Cut off any extra material. Bend into a candy cane shape.

TIPS AND VARIATIONS

*You can use this same technique to make a wreath.
Use strips that are 18 inches long.
After braiding, turn only one end back on itself.
Shape the weaving into a circle and glue the unfinished end behind the wreath.
Glue a 1-inch eyelet around the outside of the wreath.*

WHAT YOU'LL NEED

10½ inches tricolor 3-mm rattail cord
4½ inches tricolor 3-mm rattail cord
Matches
3 feet gold 2-mm rattail cord
3 feet red satin 2-mm rattail cord
1 foot gold 2-mm rattail cord
1 foot red satin 2-mm rattail cord
10 inches gold 2-mm rattail cord
White craft glue
1 spray 1-inch red carnations,
12 flowers total
Wire cutters
Hot glue mini gun
2 sprays 3-mm gold balls
Florist tape
2-piece clear plastic 4-inch egg
23-inch string 2-mm gold beads
18 gold balls, 9½ mm each
8 gold balls, 12 mm each

1. Sear the ends of the tricolor cord lengths to prevent unraveling. Apply a dab of white glue to the ends of the gold and red cord lengths to prevent unraveling.

2. Trim the bottoms from three carnations; arrange them in a circle. Hot glue the carnations together.

3. Arrange the remaining carnations in a 2½-inch-high spray. Insert a gold ball spray on either side. Bind together with florist tape. Trim stems.

4. Trim the bottoms from the carnation leaves until the leaves are 1½-inches long. Arrange the leaves around the bottom of the carnation spray and attach with hot glue.

5. Insert the carnation and leaf spray into the center of the 3-carnation circle. Hot glue into place.

6. Open the plastic egg. Center the carnation spray in the bottom of the egg half that has the inner lip. Hot glue the spray in place. Close the egg.

7. Fold the 10½-inch tricolor length of cord in half. Hot glue the middle of the cord to the egg's bottom, covering the egg seam. Using the hot glue gun, spot glue the cord up either side of the egg, covering the egg seam. (The cord will not reach to the egg's top.)

8. Using hot glue, attach one end of the 23-inch string of beads to one end of the tricolor cord near the egg's top. At 6 inches along the bead strand, glue to the other end of the tricolor cord. At 12 inches along the bead strand, glue to the first end of the tricolor cord. At 17½ inches, glue to the second end of the tricolor cord. At 23 inches, glue to the first end of the tricolor cord. You should have a double drape of beads on either side of the egg.

9. Using hot glue, attach the 4½-inch length of tricolor cord around the egg's top, touching but not covering the ends of the tricolor cord covering the egg seam.

10. Using hot glue, attach the 12-mm balls to the egg above the 4½-inch length of tricolor cord.

11. Using hot glue, attach the 9½-mm balls to cover any spaces between the larger balls.

12. Make a 1-inch loopy bow from the 3-foot lengths of red and gold cord. Use the 1-foot lengths of red and gold cord to secure the bow. Attach the loopy bow to the egg's top with an overhand knot, anchor with hot glue. (Use the 1-foot length of red cord that secured the loopy bow to tie the overhand knot.)

13. Insert the 10-inch length of gold cord through the loop at the egg's top. Tie an overhand knot about ½ inch from the open end.

COUNTRY THEME TREE

❧

Amid the hustle
and bustle of city life,
the call of the countryside
is always enticing.
Reflect a simpler
lifestyle with
country ornaments like
Holiday Holstein and
Old World St. Nick that
will make your hearth
even warmer. Add an
extra touch to your
Country tree by using the
garland, skirt, and topper
suggestions found in the
Introduction.

HOLIDAY HOLSTEIN

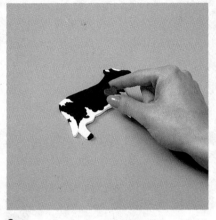

1. Paint the cow with two coats of white paint. Use black paint to place markings on the cow.

2. Glue the heart onto the cow.

3. Thread the bell onto the 3-inch length of ribbon. Glue the ribbon around the cow's neck, attaching at the back of the neck.

4. Make a 1-inch bow from the 4-inch length of ribbon. Glue the bow on top of the 3-inch length of ribbon on heart side of the cow.

5. Fold the 8-inch length of ribbon in half and tie an overhand knot ½ inch from the open end. Glue to the cow's back.

6. Glue the holly leaves and stamens just below the 8-inch piece of ribbon.

WHAT YOU'LL NEED

4-inch cow
½-inch brush
Acrylic paints: white and black
Hot glue mini gun
⅝-inch red heart
⅜-inch cowbell
3 inches red ⅛-inch ribbon
4 inches red ⅛-inch ribbon
8 inches red ⅛-inch ribbon
2 holly leaves, ½-inch leaves
2 stamens, ⅛ inch each

TIPS AND VARIATIONS

If you can't find prepainted red hearts, get unpainted ones and use red enamel paint for a shiny surface.

An encyclopedia will have photographs of many different breeds of cows; choose another breed for a different look.

1. Untwist and open all paper twist.

SANTA'S BODY:

1. Fold up ½ inch on the 7-inch side of the 4-inch paper twist. The paper should now be 3½ inches by 7 inches. This will be Santa's body. The folded side will be on the inside and bottom of Santa.

2. Make a pencil mark one inch back from the open 3-inch end on one of the 3½-inch sides.

2. Glue one 3½-inch end over the other 3½-inch end, forming a 3½-inch tube (the ½-inch fold should be on the inside of the tube).

3. Squeeze together one unfolded end and glue, forming a 3½-inch-high cone.

SANTA'S CAPE:

1. To start making Santa's cape, fold the 3-inch by 7-inch red paper twist in half, forming a 3-inch by 3½-inch rectangle.

3. Cut an arc from the pencil mark to the other corner of the open end.

4. Fold each resulting acute corner back ¼ inch to form lapel. Glue one acute corner to the top of the cone that forms the body. Wrap the cape around the cone and glue the other acute corner over the first.

5. Gather the rest of the top of the cape to the top of the cone and glue to the cone.

SANTA'S HOOD:

1. Fold the 8-inch length of gold cord in half. Make an overhand knot ½ inch from the open end. Put aside.

WHAT YOU'LL NEED

4 inches 7-inch-wide red paper twist
for body

3 inches 7-inch-wide red paper twist
for cape

2¾ inches 7-inch-wide red paper twist
for hood

7 inches 3½-inch-wide brown paper
twist for sack

Hot glue mini gun

Pencil

8 inches gold elastic cord

Wood wool

½-inch-square prewrapped present

2 candy canes, 2 inches each

Two lengths gold elastic cord,
12 inches each

Wire cutters

2 holly leaves, ½-inch leaves

¼-inch jingle bell

15-mm Santa head

2. Fold up ¾ inch on the 7-inch side of the 2¾-inch paper twist. The paper should now be 2 inches by 7 inches. This will be Santa's hood. The folded side will be on the outside and at the front of the hood.

3. With the fold on the outside, fold the hood in half.

4. Starting at the closed end and opposite the folded side, cut an arc to the edge of the fold at the open end.

5. Insert the tied gold cord into the closed end opposite the fold; this will serve as the hanger.

6. Glue the hood along the arc.

SANTA'S SACK:
1. To start making Santa's sack, fold the brown paper twist in half, forming a 3½-inch-by-3-inch rectangle. The closed end will be the bottom of the sack.

2. At the closed end, make a pencil mark about 1 inch in from the side. On each side, make a pencil mark about two inches from the closed end.

3. Cut an arc from one mark on the closed end to one mark on the side. Repeat for the other 2 marks. This will be the curved bottom of Santa's sack.

4. Glue the curved sides together and turn the sack inside out.

5. Stuff bag with wood wool.

6. Gather the sack about 1 inch from the top.

7. Glue the prewrapped present in the opening of the sack. Glue the candy canes in place behind the present.

8. Tie the two 12-inch lengths of gold cord around the gathered opening of the sack. Tie a 1-inch bow at the front of the sack.

9. Trim the stems from the holly leaves. Glue the leaves just below the bow.

10. Glue the jingle bell where the holly leaves meet. Set sack aside.

PUTTING IT ALL TOGETHER:

1. Glue Santa's head on top of the cone that forms the body and cape.

2. Glue the hood in place at Santa's neck.

3. Compress and roll a clump of wood wool around in your hands. Form a beard around the bottom of Santa's face and glue into place.

4. Do the same with another clump of wood wool to form Santa's hair. Glue into place.

5. Glue the hood to the top of the hair.

6. Glue the sack, at an angle, to the front of Santa.

COUNTRY CHRISTMAS GOOSE

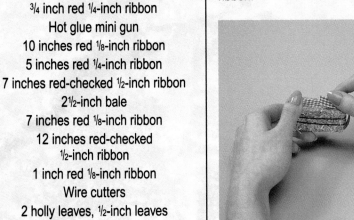

WHAT YOU'LL NEED

2¾-inch goose
¾ inch red ¼-inch ribbon
Hot glue mini gun
10 inches red ⅛-inch ribbon
5 inches red ¼-inch ribbon
7 inches red-checked ½-inch ribbon
2½-inch bale
7 inches red ⅛-inch ribbon
12 inches red-checked
⅛-inch ribbon
1 inch red ⅛-inch ribbon
Wire cutters
2 holly leaves, ½-inch leaves
2 stamens, ⅛ inch each

1. This type of goose often comes with a felt bow on its neck. Carefully remove the felt bow but leave the felt neck band.

2. Cover the felt band with the ¾-inch piece of red ¼-inch ribbon. Fold the 10-inch length of red ⅛-inch ribbon in half. Glue the open end to the ¼-inch ribbon at the back of the neck.

3. Make a 1-inch bow from the 5-inch piece of red ¼-inch ribbon. Glue the bow to the back of the goose's neck on top of the neck band and the ⅛-inch ribbon.

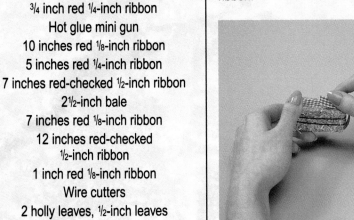

4. Glue one end of the 7-inch length of red-checked ribbon in the center of one side of the bale. Wrap the ribbon around the bale and glue the other end over the first end.

5. Center and wrap the 7-inch piece of ⅛-inch ribbon around the 7-inch checked ribbon. Glue in place.

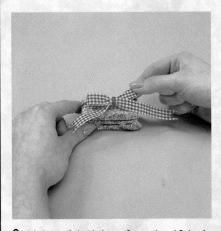

6. Make a 3-inch bow from the 12-inch length of red-checked ribbon. Cover the center knot of the bow with the 1-inch length of ⅛-inch ribbon. Glue the bow to the side of the bale, covering the glued ends of the ribbons wrapped around the bale.

7. Trim the stems from the holly leaves. Glue the leaves into the knot of the bow. Trim the stems from the stamens and glue the stamens onto the holly leaves.

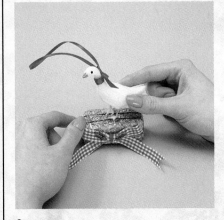

8. Clip the wires protruding from the goose's feet. Glue the feet to the top of the bale; the goose should be turned slightly to the side of the bale with the bow.

BUTTONS 'N' EYELET WREATH

1. Fold ⅛-inch ribbon in half. Tie an overhand knot ½ inch from the open end. Using the glue gun, glue the folded end to the rear of the wreath.

2. Using the glue gun, glue the eyelet to the back of the wreath. The ends of the eyelet should overlap.

3. Using white glue, arrange the ⅝-inch buttons around the wreath in a random arrangement.

4. Using white glue, arrange the ⅜-inch buttons randomly around the wreath.

WHAT YOU'LL NEED

8 inches eggshell ⅛-inch ribbon
Hot glue mini gun
4-inch grapevine wreath
12 inches eggshell 1-inch eyelet
White craft glue
5 white buttons, ⅝ inch each
20 white buttons, ⅜ inch each

TIPS AND VARIATIONS

You don't need to buy new buttons; the ones you have collected over the years will be fine.

For variety, use colored buttons and a complementary color eyelet.

1. Make a 2½-inch bow from the ½-inch ribbon. Glue the bow to the top of the buttermold.

2. Take apart the holly pick and clip stems. Glue the leaves in the knot of the bow. Do the same with the stamens.

3. Make a ¾-inch bow from the ⅛-inch ribbon. Glue to the bottom of the buttermold.

4. Fold the elastic cord in half and tie an overhand knot ½ inch from the open end. Glue the cord to the rear of the 2½-inch bow.

WHAT YOU'LL NEED

12 inches blue-checked ½-inch ribbon
Hot glue mini gun
Heart-shaped tin buttermold
3-leaved glazed holly pick, ½-inch leaves
2 stamens, ⅛ inch each
Wire cutters
2 inches blue-checked ⅛-inch ribbon
8 inches gold elastic cord

TIPS AND VARIATIONS

You can find tin buttermolds in cake decorating or candy supply stores. Try a variety of shapes to make a whole series of ornaments.

Jute Twist

What You'll Need

2 red grape sprays,
3½ inches each

Hot glue mini gun

3 feet ⅛-inch jute

2 lengths ⅛-inch jute,
10 inches each

8 inches ⅛-inch jute

1. Bend one spray into an arc with each end pointed left. Bend the other spray into an arc with each end pointed right.

2. Glue the stems of the sprays together.

3. Make a loopy bow from the 3-foot length of jute. Tie the center of the bow with the two lengths of 10-inch jute.

4. Glue the bow to the stems of the sprays.

5. Fold the 8-inch length of jute in half. Glue the open end to the rear of the stems.

Tips and Variations

You can use any color grape you wish. Be sure the spray is three to four inches long; a larger spray may be too heavy for the tree limb.

JOY TO THE WORLD

1. Cut a small hole in the center of the batting. Cut the batting into an uneven circle.

2. Pass the ornament's hanger cord through the hole in batting. Glue the batting into place at the North Pole.

3. Glue the penguin just in front of the hanger cord. Glue the trees to either side of the penguin.

TIPS AND VARIATIONS

Instead of a penguin, use a picture of your child. Find a photograph of your child that is about 1½ inches by 2 inches. Using a craft knife, cut your child out from the rest of the photograph. Glue the outline to a thin piece of cardboard. Trim any excess cardboard.

WHAT YOU'LL NEED

Scissors
2-inch square polyester batting
3-inch globe ornament
Hot glue mini gun
¾-inch penguin
2 sisal trees, 2 inches each

BOUNTIFUL SANTA

WHAT YOU'LL NEED

Scissors

Felt squares: red and black

White craft glue

Foam ball, 3-inch diameter

Sequin pins

Wooden ball, 30-mm diameter

½-inch brush

Acrylic paints: white, black, blue, and red

White craft fur

9 inches red ¹⁄₁₆-inch ribbon

¼-inch white pom-pom

Hot glue mini gun

5/0 sable brush

2 holly leaves, ½-inch

⅛-inch stamen

Wire cutters

2 candy canes, 2½-inches

10 inches plaid ⅜-inch ribbon

Frosted sisal tree, 3½ inches

GETTING STARTED:

1. Cut out the patterns for "Bountiful Santa." See page 64 for the patterns. See Introduction, page 5, for instructions on cutting out patterns.

2. Following the pattern for Santa's body, cut 7 pieces from the red felt. Apply white craft glue to the foam ball. Attach the felt pieces to the ball and hold in place with pins. The pieces should be evenly distributed around the ball and overlap slightly. After the glue has dried, remove the pins. Set aside.

3. Paint the wooden ball white with the ½-inch brush. Set aside until the paint has dried.

4. From the craft fur, cut the following pieces: 1 circle, 2-inch diameter, for the bottom; 1 belt, 10 inches by ¾ inch; 2 cuffs, 1½ inches by ½ inch each; 1 chest, 2½ inches by ¾ inch; 1 collar, 5 inches by ¾ inch; 1 trim for hat, 6 inches by ½ inch; 1 beard, follow pattern from page 64.

5. Following the pattern, cut 2 mittens and 1 belt buckle from the black felt. Following the pattern, cut 2 arms and 1 hat from the red felt.

SANTA'S HAT:

1. To make Santa's hat, apply white glue to one straight side of the cut red felt. Overlap glued straight side to other straight side, forming a cone.

2. Using white glue, attach the trim for the hat to the bottom edge of the cone.

3. Fold the red ribbon in half. Insert the open end into the top of the cone. Attach the ribbon in place using white glue.

4. While holding the ribbon along the seam of the hat, use white glue to attach the white pom-pom over the ribbon to the top of the cone. Set aside.

PUTTING IT ALL TOGETHER:
1. Use the white glue to assemble Santa. Glue in the following order: circle to bottom of ball (where the body pieces overlap), belt around middle of ball, mittens to straight ends of arms, cuffs over ends of mittens and arms, rounded ends of arms to either side of top of ball, chest piece from top of ball to belt, and belt buckle to center front of belt.

2. Using hot glue, attach the wooden ball to the top of the foam ball where the body pieces overlap.

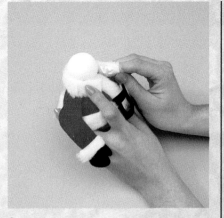

3. Fold the collar piece in half to find the middle of the collar. Using white glue, glue the middle of the collar to the back of Santa's head where it joins Santa's body. Place the front points of the collar under Santa's chin.

4. Using white glue, attach Santa's beard.

5. Using white glue, attach Santa's hat. Be sure the hat seam is toward the rear.

6. Using the 5/0 brush and acrylic paints, paint Santa's face as shown.

7. Trim the stems from the holly leaves and stamen. Using white glue, attach the leaves and stamen to Santa's beard beneath his right cheek.

8. Cross the candy canes and glue them together with hot glue. Glue the crossed candy canes to Santa's right mitten with hot glue.

9. Curve the right mitten tip and glue it (with hot glue) to Santa's buckle.

10. Make a 1³/₄-inch bow from the plaid ribbon. Using hot glue, attach the bow to the stem of the tree.

11. Using hot glue, attach the tree to the left side of Santa's belt buckle. Then glue Santa's left mitten tip to the tree's base.

WHAT YOU'LL NEED

7-inch by 8-inch piece 14-count white
Aida cloth
6-strand cotton embroidery floss
(see color key)
#24 tapestry needle
Iron-on backing
3-inch by 4-inch piece red felt
7 inches red ⅛-inch ribbon
5 inches red ⅛-inch ribbon
White craft glue

Color key:

Black		310 DMC
Red		321 DMC
White		Blanc Neige DMC
Yellow		742 DMC
Gold		729 DMC
Light Brown		51c Coats
Dark Brown		81b Coats
Pink		948 DMC
Blue		312 DMC
Light Tan		3024 DMC

Stitch count: 33w × 46h
Finished size: 2.36 × 3.29 inches

1. Find the center of the Aida. Starting at the center of the design, using 2 strands, stitch according to the chart. For the candy cane, make the first stitch of the cross-stitch in white and the second stitch in red.

2. When all cross-stitching is done, backstitch around Santa's beard and fur using 1 strand of black. Backstitch around Rudolph's antlers, paws, and tail with 1 strand of dark brown. Backstitch around part of Santa's boot with 1 strand of white. Using 2 strands of blue, make French knots for Santa's eyes. Using 2 strands of black, make French knots for Rudolph's eyes. Using 2 strands of white, stitch snowflakes in long stitches as indicated in the chart.

3. Following the manufacturer's instructions, apply the iron-on backing to the felt. Trim the felt to the size and shape of the cross-stitched area.

4. Fold the 7-inch length of ribbon in half. Place the open end to the top center of the back of the felt piece. Following the instructions of the manufacturer of the iron-on backing, affix the felt to the back of the cross-stitch.

5. Trim the Aida cloth to within ⅜ inch of the edge of the cross-stitching. Fringe the Aida cloth by pulling threads from all four sides until the edge of the cross-stitching is reached.

6. Make a ¾-inch bow from the 5-inch length of ribbon. Glue to the top center of the ornament.

DINOSAUR IN DECEMBER

Texas Santa Patterns

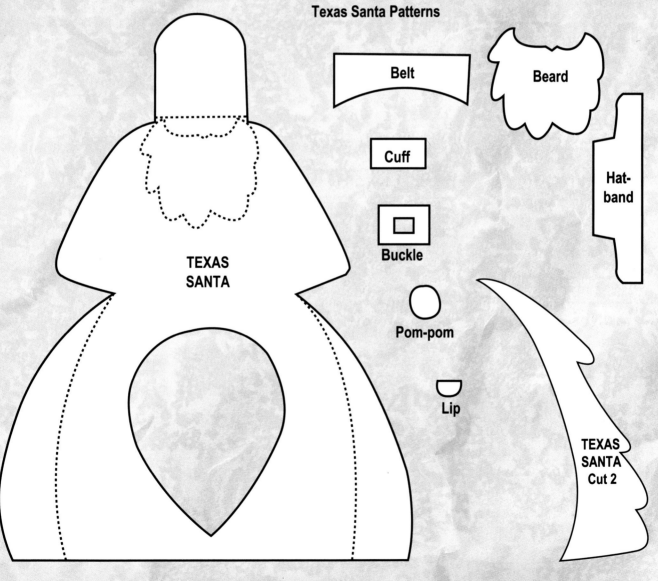

Belt

Beard

Cuff

Hat-band

Buckle

TEXAS
SANTA

Pom-pom

Lip

TEXAS
SANTA
Cut 2

·············· **Placement Lines**

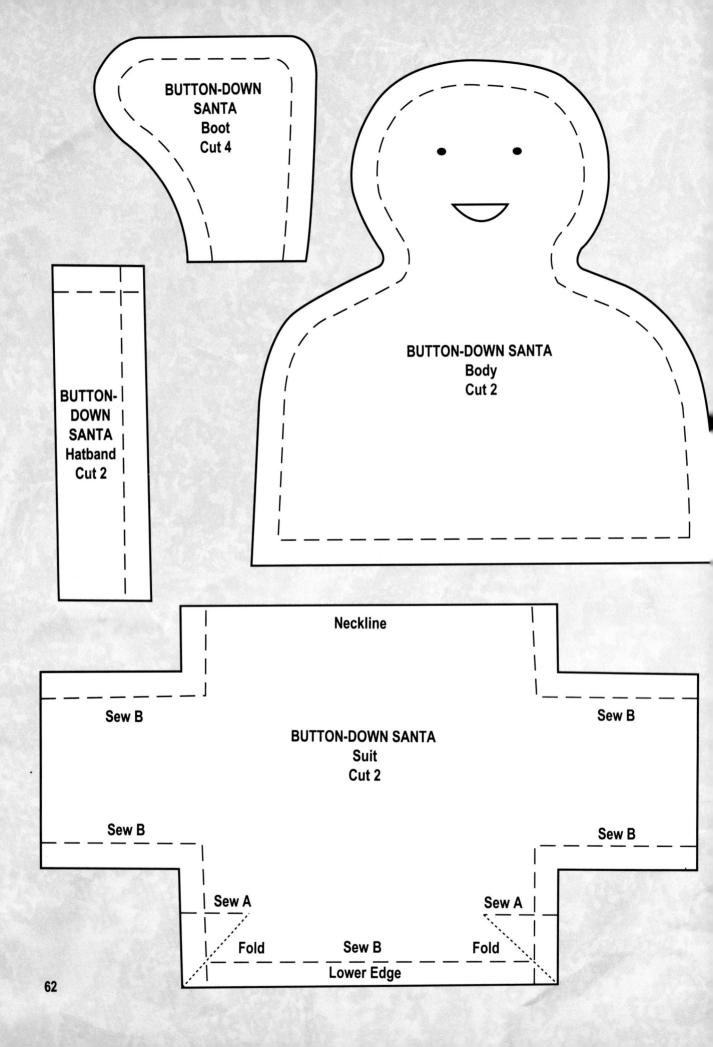

BUTTON-DOWN
SANTA
Boot
Cut 4

BUTTON-DOWN SANTA
Body
Cut 2

BUTTON-
DOWN
SANTA
Hatband
Cut 2

Neckline

Sew B

Sew B

BUTTON-DOWN SANTA
Suit
Cut 2

Sew B

Sew B

Sew A

Sew A

Fold

Sew B

Fold

Lower Edge

62

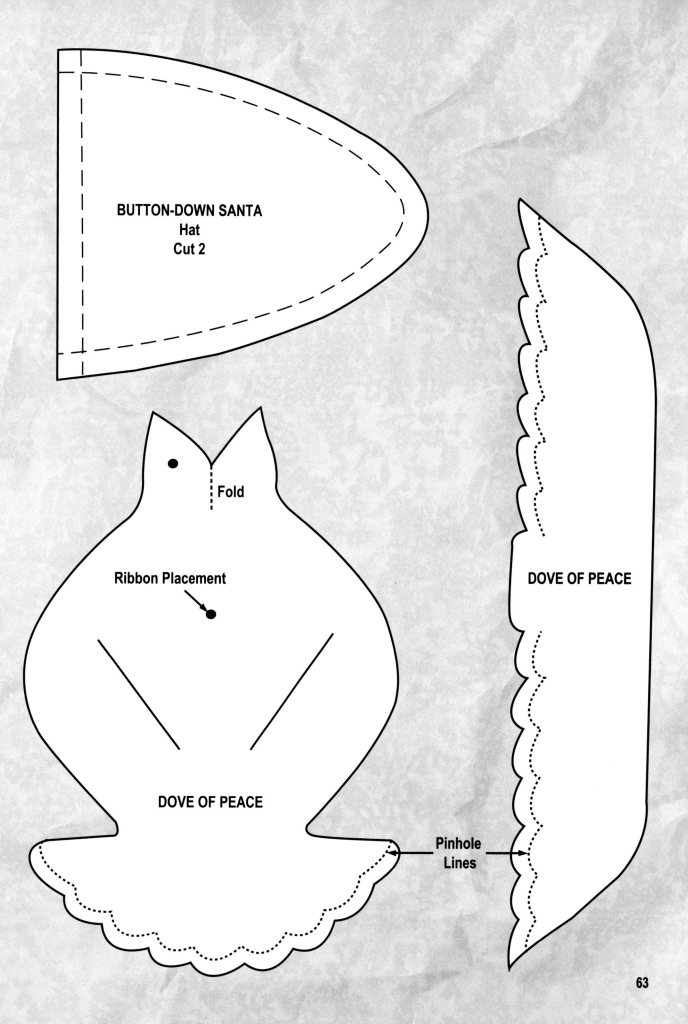

BUTTON-DOWN SANTA
Hat
Cut 2

Fold

Ribbon Placement

DOVE OF PEACE

DOVE OF PEACE

Pinhole
Lines

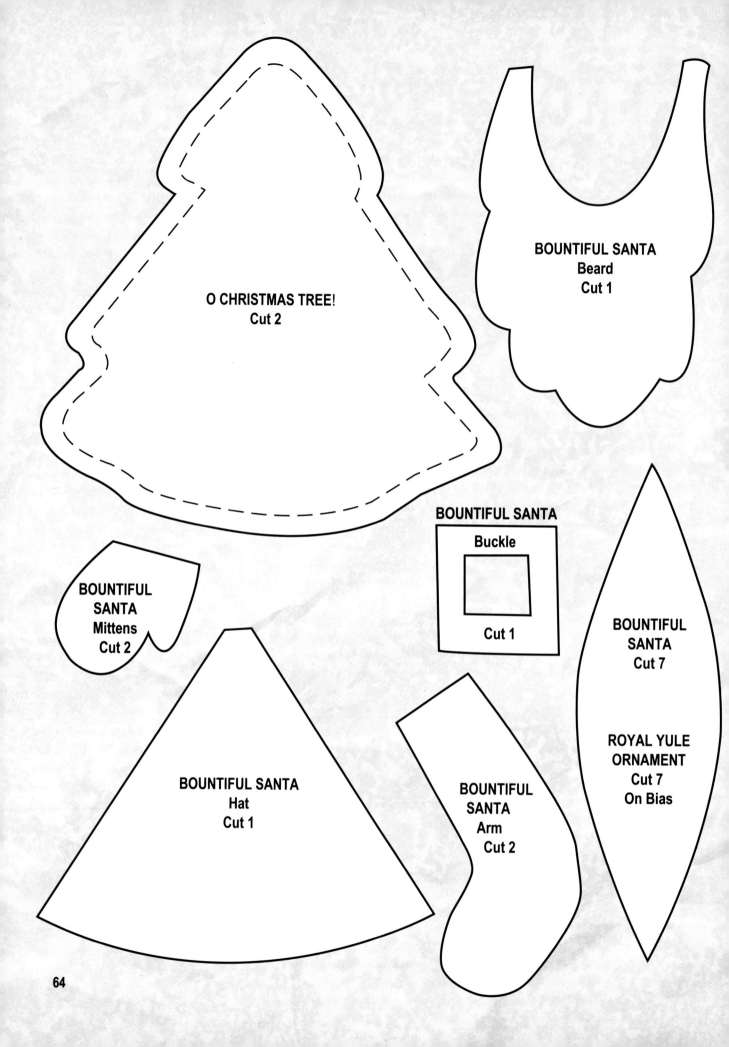

O CHRISTMAS TREE!
Cut 2

BOUNTIFUL SANTA
Beard
Cut 1

BOUNTIFUL SANTA
Buckle
Cut 1

BOUNTIFUL
SANTA
Mittens
Cut 2

BOUNTIFUL SANTA
Hat
Cut 1

BOUNTIFUL
SANTA
Arm
Cut 2

BOUNTIFUL
SANTA
Cut 7

ROYAL YULE
ORNAMENT
Cut 7
On Bias

The CHRISTMAS crafts book

Contributing Writer and Consultant

Lynda Scott Musante

PUBLICATIONS INTERNATIONAL, LTD.

Louis Weber, C.E.O.
Publications International, Ltd.
7373 North Cicero Avenue
Lincolnwood, Illinois 60646

Permission is never granted for commercial purposes.

Manufactured in U.S.A.

8 7 6 5 4 3 2 1

ISBN 0-7853-0538-6

Photography: Sam Griffith Studios and Siede/Preis Photography
Models: Desiree Mertz/Stewart Talent Management Corporation. Cindy Cottrell and Anita White/Royal Model Management.

Thanks to THE BEADERY, Bedford Industries, Inc., Black & Decker, Maria Buscemi, Delta/Shiva Technical Coatings, Inc., The DMC Corporation, The Dow Chemical Company, Karen's Kreations, Kreinik Manufacturing, Inc., MPR Associates, Inc., Nifty Publishing Company, and Tulip/Polymerics, Inc.

CONTENTS

INTRODUCTION

Christmas is the season that evokes cherished memories for everyone—traditional family celebrations, the warmth and cheer of a jolly Santa Claus, or a child's wonderful anticipation of a magical time. It is also a chance to be surrounded by all the beauty we find around and within ourselves as we try to re-create childhood memories out of family traditions.

Imagine your home transformed with some of the lovely items found in the following pages! Handmade decorations and gifts are a wonderful way to create impressions that will be cherished memories next Christmas. Friends and family will find your gifts extra special when they know you made them yourself.

The projects in this book include a wide variety of techniques and methods. Take a moment and look through the pages. Crafting at Christmastime is a wonderful way to escape the crowded shopping malls and the mad race to find that "perfect" gift. Now you'll be able to make something wonderful for many on your gift list right at home. Each project has complete step-by-step instructions and photos to help make everything easy to understand.

We hope you enjoy creating these projects. They are for all skill levels and interests. You'll find that many of the projects use basic items you already have around your home. Once you begin, you'll see that creating your own holiday decorations and gifts is a satisfying and relaxing way to get ready for the holidays.

JEWELRY MAKING AND TOOLS

Although the jewelry projects in this book look sophisticated, most are made by gluing and wiring. You'll need some tools to make them, including wire cutters, needle-nose pliers, and tweezers. A craft knife may also come in handy. Jewelry findings is a term for a variety of ready-made metal components used as attachments and fastenings to assemble a piece of jewelry. They are usually made of inexpensive metal. Findings include pin backs, earring findings, barrel clasps, jump rings, and beading wire. All of these items are easily found in your local craft or hobby store.

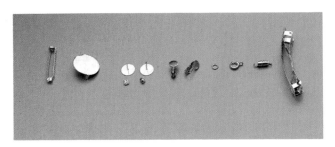

Left to right: bar pin back, disk pin back, disk-style pierced earring posts/earnuts, clip-style earring backs with flat pads, spring ring with jump ring, barrel clasp, spring barrette

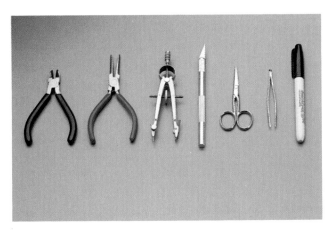

Left to right: wire cutters, needle-nose pliers, compass, craft knife, scissors, tweezers, permanent ink marker

CROSS-STITCH

Cross-stitch is traditionally worked on an "even-weave" cloth that has vertical and horizontal threads of equal thickness and spacing. Six-strand embroidery floss is used for most stitching; there are also many beautiful threads that can be used to enhance the appearance of the stitching. Finishing and framing a counted cross-stitch piece will truly complete your work. There are many options in framing—just visit your local craft shop or framing gallery.

Basic Supplies

Fabric: The most common even-weave fabric is 14-count Aida cloth. The weave of this fabric creates distinct squares that make stitching very easy for the beginner. The projects in this book are stitched on 14-count Aida cloth.

Needles, Hoops, and Scissors: A blunt-end or tapestry needle is used for counted cross-stitch. A #24 needle is the recommended size for stitching on 14-count Aida cloth. You may use an embroidery hoop while stitching—just be sure to remove it when not working on your project. A small pair of sharp scissors is a definite help when working with embroidery floss.

Floss: Six-strand cotton embroidery floss is most commonly used, and it's usually cut into 18-inch lengths for stitching. Use two of the six strands for stitching on 14-count Aida cloth. Also use two strands for backstitching.

Preparing to Stitch

The patterns in this book will tell you what size the overall stitched area will be when completed. It will also tell you what size piece of Aida cloth to use.

To locate the center of the design, lightly fold your fabric in half and in half again. Find the center of the chart by following the arrows on the sides.

Reading the chart is easy, since each square on the chart equals one stitch on the fabric. The colors correspond to the floss numbers listed in the color key. Select a color and stitch all of that color within an area. Begin by holding the thread ends behind the fabric until secured or covered over with two or three stitches. You may skip a few stitches on the back of the material, but do not run the thread from one area to another behind a section that will not be stitched in the finished piece. If your thread begins to twist, drop the needle and allow the thread to untwist. It is important to the final appearance of the project to keep an even tension when pulling your stitches through so that all of your stitches will have a uniform look. To end a thread, weave or run the thread under several stitches on the back side. Cut the ends close to the fabric.

Each counted cross-stitch is represented by a colored square on the project's chart. For horizontal rows, work the stitches in two steps, i.e., all of the left to right stitches and then all of the right to left stitches (see Figure A). For vertical rows, work each complete stitch as shown in Figure B. Three-quarter stitches are often used when the design requires two colors in one square or to allow more detail in the pattern (see Figure C). The backstitch is often used to outline or create letters, and is shown by bold lines on the patterns. Backstitch is usually worked after the pattern is completed (see Figure D).

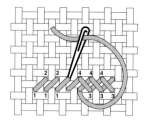

Fig. A
Cross-stitch

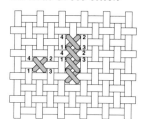

Fig. B
Vertical Cross-stitch

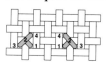

Fig. C
Three-quarter Stitches

Fig. D
Backstitching

PLASTIC CANVAS

Plastic canvas allows for three-dimensional stitchery projects to be constructed. Stitching on plastic canvas is easy to do, easy on the eyes, and easy on the pocketbook, too.

Basic Supplies
Plastic Canvas: Canvas is most widely available by the sheet. Stitch all the pieces of a project on the same brand of plastic canvas to ensure that the meshes will match when you join them together. Plastic canvas comes in several counts or mesh sizes (number of stitches to the inch) and numerous sizes of sheets. Specialty sizes and shapes such as circles are also available. Most canvas is clear, although up to 24 colors are available. Colored canvas is used when parts of the project remain unstitched. Seven-count canvas comes in four weights—standard; a thinner, flexible weight; a stiffer, rigid weight; and a softer weight made especially for bending and curved projects. Designs can be stitched on any mesh count—the resulting size of the project is the only thing that will be affected. The smaller the count number, the larger the project will be, since the count number refers to the number of stitches per inch. Therefore, 7-count has seven stitches per inch, while 14-count has 14. A 14-count project will be half the size of a 7-count project if two identical projects were stitched on 7-count and 14-count canvas.

Needles: Needle size is determined by the count size of the plastic canvas you are using. Patterns generally call for a #18 needle for stitching on 7-count plastic canvas, a #16 or #18 for 10-count canvas, and a #22 or #24 for stitching on 14-count plastic canvas.

Yarns: A wide variety of yarns may be used. The most common is worsted weight (or 4-ply). Acrylic yarns are less expensive and washable; wool may also be used. Several companies produce specialty yarns for plastic canvas work. These cover the canvas well and will not "pill" as some acrylics do. Sport weight yarn (or 3-ply) and embroidery floss are often used on 10-count canvas. Use 12 strands or double the floss thickness for 10-count canvas and 6 strands for stitching on 14-count canvas. On 14-count plastic canvas, many of the specialty metallic threads made for cross-stitch can be used to highlight and enhance your project.

Cutting Out Your Project

Many plastic canvas projects are dimensional—a shape has to be cut out and stitched. Scissors or a craft knife are recommended.

Preparing to Stitch

Cut your yarn to a 36-inch length. Begin by holding the yarn end behind the fabric until secured or covered over with two or three stitches. To end a length, weave or run the yarn under several stitches on the back side. Cut the end close to the canvas. The continental stitch is the most commonly used stitch to cover plastic canvas. Decorative stitches will add interest and texture to your project. As in cross-stitch, if your yarn begins to twist, drop the needle and allow the yarn to untwist. It is important to the final appearance of the project to keep an even tension when pulling your stitches through so that all of your stitches have a uniform look. Do not pull your stitches too tight, since this causes gaps in your stitching and allows the canvas to show through between your stitches. Also do not carry one color yarn across too many rows of another

color on the back—the carried color may show through to the front of your project. Do not stitch the outer edge of the canvas until the other stitching is complete. If the project is a single piece of canvas, overcast the outer edge with the color specified. If there are two or more pieces, follow the pattern instructions for assembly.

Cleaning

If projects are stitched with acrylic yarn, they may be washed by hand using warm or cool water and a mild detergent. Place on a terry cloth towel to air dry. Do not place in a dryer or dry clean.

The following stitches are used in plastic canvas:

The **continental stitch** is the most common stitch. Your needle comes up at 1 and all odd-numbered holes and goes down at 2 and all even-numbered holes.

The **French knot** is used for accents, such as eyes. Bring your needle up at one hole and wrap the yarn clockwise around the needle once. Holding the yarn firmly with the nonstitching hand, insert the needle in the hole to the right and slowly pull yarn through.

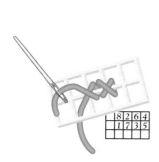

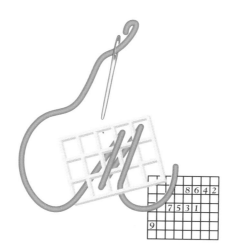

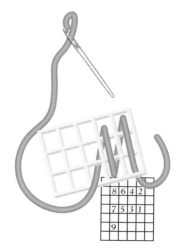

The **cross-stitch** is worked as a diagonal stitch in one direction and then in the opposite direction, forming a cross. If making several stitches in a row, work all stitches in one direction first, then cross them working in the other direction. The tip strands of yarn should always be slanted the same way. Your needle comes up at 1 and all odd-numbered holes and goes down at 2 and all even-numbered holes.

The **slanted gobelin stitch** is almost the same as the continental stitch except you skip a row (or rows) of canvas. Your needle comes up at 1 and all odd-numbered holes and goes down at 2 and all even-numbered holes. For the next row, your needle comes up at 9 and goes down at 7.

The **straight gobelin stitch** is similar to the slanted gobelin, except it is straight up and down. Your needle comes up at 1 and all odd-numbered holes and goes down at 2 and all even-numbered holes. The second row is the same as for the slanted gobelin stitch.

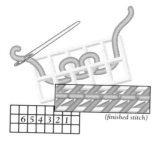

(finished stitch)

The **back-stitch** is worked on top of a stitched piece to outline and define areas. The needle comes up at 1 and goes down at the hole directly to the right; then the needle comes up at 2 and goes down at the hole directly to the right (hole 1). The back-stitch may also be worked skipping rows; each hole need not be stitched in if the pattern allows.

The **overcast stitch** is used to finish edges; it may be worked in either direction. The needle goes down at the numbered holes, and the yarn wraps over the edge of the canvas. Make sure to cover the canvas completely—you may go through the same hole two or more times.

WEARABLES

You'll find fabric painting to be fast, easy, and fun. With the latest development in fabric paints, using basic dimensional paints is almost as easy as writing with a ballpoint pen. Some of the painting projects will require a brush—we'll tell you what type of brush you'll need in the project's materials list.

Using a Shirt Board

You'll need a commercially purchased shirt board, or you can make your own by cutting corrugated cardboard into the shape of a flattened T-shirt about ½ inch smaller than the shirt you'll be using. Cover it with wax paper and insert it into the item you'll be working on—it will prevent paint from bleeding through and make it easier for you to transport a project with wet paint. Make sure the waxed side is under the surface you want to paint.

Paints

Each of the projects will specify the type of paints required. Only dimensional and embellished paints, which are especially formulated to use on fabric, are used.

Basic Guidelines for Wearables

1. Prewash fabric and sweatshirt without using any softeners. Softeners prevent the paint from bonding completely with the fibers. Press out any wrinkles.
2. If you're right-handed, work on your project from the upper left-hand corner to the lower right-hand corner. Paint all colors as you go. This will prevent you from accidentally smearing the paint with your elbow or hand.
3. When using dimensional paints, pick up the tube of paint with the cap on and shake the paint down into the tip to remove any air bubbles each time you use a color. Place a paint bottle down on its side between uses.
4. Hold your dimensional paint bottle like a ballpoint pen. Squeeze gently to push out paint. Work quickly and smoothly. Moving too slowly often results in a "bumpy" appearance.
5. When using dimensional glitter paint, be sure to draw a line of paint that is thick enough to carry the glitter.
6. Allow paints to dry at least six to eight hours before touching. Allow 36 to 48 hours for paint to be completely cured before wearing.

Caring For Your Wearable

Hand wash or wash in lukewarm water—NOT COLD!!—in delicate/knit cycle. Cold water will crack the paint. Tumble dry on low for a few minutes to remove wrinkles, then remove and lay flat to dry. Do not wash in Woolite or other delicate care wash products.

A WORD ABOUT GLUE

Glue can be a sticky subject when you don't use the right one for the job. There are many different glues in the craft market today, each formulated for a different crafting purpose. The following are ones to be familiar with:

White Glue: This may be used as an all-purpose glue—it dries clear and flexible. It is often referred to as craft glue or tacky glue. Tacky on contact, it allows you to put two items together without a lot of setup time required. Use for most projects, especially ones involving wood, plastics, some fabrics, and cardboard.

Thin-Bodied Glues: Use these glues when your project requires a smooth, thin layer of glue. Thin-bodied glues work well on some fabrics and papers.

Fabric Glue: This type of glue is formulated to bond with fabric fibers and withstand repeated washing. Use this kind of glue for attaching rhinestones and/or other charms to fabric projects. Some glues require heat-setting. Check the bottle for complete instructions.

Hot Melt Glue: Formed into cylindrical sticks, this glue is inserted into a hot temperature glue gun and heated to liquid state. Depending on the type of glue gun used, the glue is forced out through the gun's nozzle by either pushing on the end of the glue stick or squeezing a trigger. Use clear glue sticks for projects using wood, fabrics, most plastics, ceramics, and cardboard. When using any glue gun, be careful of the nozzle and the freshly applied glue. Apply glue to the piece being attached. Work with small areas at a time so that the glue doesn't dry before being pressed into place.

Low Melt Glue: This is similar to hot melt glues in that it is formed into sticks and requires a glue gun to be used. Low melt glues are used for projects that would be damaged by heat. Examples include foam, balloons, and metallic ribbons. Low melt glue sticks are oval-shaped and can only be used in a low temperature glue gun.

SPARKLING HOLIDAY JEWELRY

You'll be the talk of the town in these glittering, bejeweled accessories. Their sophisticated elegance will accent any outfit. Acrylic and foiled beads and stones come in a wide variety of colors and styles. After you try these projects you'll find that you'll be able to change the look of an accessory just by changing the color or the style of stones you choose.

1. Glue one Dark Ruby and three Emerald Holly Leaves on one Round Crystal Mirror as shown.

2. Glue a second layer of five Ruby Leaves on top of the leaves in Step 1.

3. Glue five Round Gold Beads clustered on top of the leaves.

4. Glue an earring post back or clip back to the back of the mirror. Repeat all steps to make a second earring.

Courtesy of The Beadery Craft Products.

MATERIALS

- **Two 15mm Round Acrylic Mirrors—Crystal**

- **Twelve 19 × 10.5mm Foiled Holly Leaves— Dark Ruby**

- **Six 19 × 10.5mm Foiled Holly Leaves— Emerald**

- **White glue or low temperature glue gun and glue sticks**

- **Ten 24K gold washed 4mm Round Acrylic Beads**

- **One pair of earring posts and backs or clip backs**

HOLIDAY MAGIC PIN

MATERIALS

• **One 40mm Round Acrylic Mirror—Crystal**

• **Twenty-four 19 × 10.5mm Foiled Holly Leaves—Emerald**

• **White glue or low temperature glue gun and glue sticks**

• **Fifteen 5mm Round Acrylic Faceted Stones— Ruby**

• **5 inches of red and green ⅜-inch ribbon**

• **3 inches of 24-gauge gold craft wire**

• **One pin back**

1. Glue 12 Holly Leaves around the edge of the mirror.

2. Glue 12 more Holly Leaves on top of the first layer.

3. Glue the Round Ruby Stones on top in clusters of three.

4. Fold the ribbon into thirds. Wrap the wire around the middle of the ribbon. Twist the wire ends together in the back, three times. Trim the wire ends and lay them flat. Trim the ribbon ends. Glue the bow to the front of the wreath. Glue the pin back to the back of the mirror.

Courtesy of The Beadery Craft Products.

1. Glue the Crystal Holly Leaves and Ruby Pear-shaped Stones down on the hairband, evenly spaced. Use large Ruby Pear-shaped Stones in the center cluster only.

2. Glue the Emerald Holly Leaves in place.

3. Glue the Topaz Stones in place.

Courtesy of The Beadery Craft Products.

MATERIALS

- **One 1¼-inch width black adult size hairband**

- **Ten 19 × 10.5mm Foiled Holly Leaves—Crystal**

- **Eight 10 × 7mm Pear-shaped Acrylic Faceted Stones—Ruby**

- **White glue, low temperature glue gun and glue sticks, or fabric glue**

- **Two 13 × 9mm Pear-shaped Acrylic Faceted Stones—Ruby**

- **Twenty 14 × 7.5mm Foiled Holly Leaves—Emerald**

- **Five 8mm Round Acrylic Faceted Stones—Topaz**

HERALD ANGEL PIN

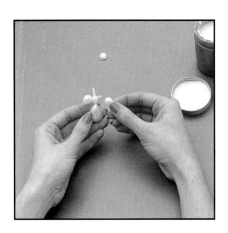

1. Cut two pieces of index card: one ⅛ inch by 1½ inches and the second ⅛ inch by ¾ inch. Glue them in a cross formation. Glue the Pearl Cabochons on top of the cross.

2. Starting under one wing, carefully glue the gold braid around the Pearl Cabochons in a figure-eight fashion. Hide the ends of the cord under the crossover between two beads.

3. Glue the 18mm Topaz Faceted Stone under the angel's head. Glue the three Emerald Navettes, three Dark Amethyst Cabochons, and two Ruby Oval Faceted Stones to the edges of the Topaz mirrors. Glue the mirrors to the underside of the angel. Glue the pin back to the back of the entire piece.

Courtesy of The Beadery Craft Products.

MATERIALS

- **One 3 × 5-inch index card or similar card stock**

- **Ruler**

- **Scissors**

- **White glue or low temperature glue gun and glue sticks**

- **One 25 × 18mm Pear-shaped Acrylic Cabochon—Antique White Pearl**

- **Two 15 × 11mm Pear-shaped Acrylic Cabochons—Antique White Pearl**

- **One 12mm Round Acrylic Cabochon—Antique White Pearl**

- **One 10 × 8mm Oval Acrylic Cabochon—Antique White Pearl**

- **15 inches of #50 gold braided cord**

- **One 18mm Round Acrylic Faceted Stone—Topaz**

- **One 25mm Round Acrylic Mirror—Topaz**

- **One 18mm Round Acrylic Mirror—Topaz**

- **Three 8 × 4mm Navette Acrylic Faceted Stones—Emerald**

- **Three 5mm Round Acrylic Cabochons—Dark Amethyst**

- **Two 6 × 4mm Oval Acrylic Faceted Stones—Ruby**

- **One pin back**

HOLIDAY PLAID JEWELRY

The red and green holiday plaid of this necklace and accessory set just shouts "Christmas!" Matched with a festive skirt and blouse, these accessories are sure to draw compliments. They are also very versatile—just think of how you can change their look with different fabrics or added beads. You should let your imagination go wild!

NECKLACE

1. Fold the ribbon in half, right sides together, forming a tube 2 inches wide by 36 inches long. Sew a ¼- to ½-inch seam on the long edge with a sewing machine or by hand using very small stitches. Turn the tube right-side out.

2. Fold in the raw edge ¼ inch on one end of the tube. Hand-stitch close to the edge and pull the stitches to close up; knot to secure. Stitch one jump ring to the end and cut the thread. Leave the jump ring open. Fill the tube with 22 balls.

3. Push the first ball down to the gathered end. Wrap beading wire around the ribbon tube next to the first ball. Twist the ends together to secure the wire. Position the second ball as close as possible to the first ball. Bring the wire down under the second ball and wrap it around the tube two to three times. (Do not cut the wire. Each wrap will be connected.) Continue in this manner until you reach the last ball. Do not wrap this one yet. Cut the tube, leaving a 1-inch tail from the end of the last ball. Fold under the raw edges at the open end of the tube, and hand-stitch close to the edge. Pull the stitches to close the end around the last ball and to gather. Stitch the remaining jump ring to the end, leaving the ring open. Cut the thread.

MATERIALS

- **36 × 4-inch piece of red and green plaid ribbon**

- **Ruler**

- **Scissors**

- **Thread**

- **Needle or sewing machine**

- **Two 5mm or larger jump rings**

- **Twenty-two ⅞-inch balls of STYROFOAM brand plastic foam**

- **10 yards of #28 gauge green beading wire**

- **One 6mm or larger spring ring**

- **Needle-nose pliers**

4. Bring the beading wire up over the last ball and slip it through the open jump ring. Bring it down on the other side of the ball and wrap it two to three times around the bottom of the ball, over the previously wrapped area. Continue wrapping the balls and slipping the wire through the jump rings at each end of the necklace until you have wrapped each ball five times. Keep the wires separated.

5. Attach a spring ring to the jump ring. Close the jump ring with needle-nose pliers.

6. Continue wrapping the necklace until you reach the tenth ball. Wrap the wire twice more between balls ten and eleven. Repeat this procedure with the next two balls, then finish wrapping the remaining balls as in Step 4. You will now have six wires on each ball.

BARRETTE

MATERIALS

- **Two ⅞-inch balls of STYROFOAM brand plastic foam**

- **Craft knife**

- **10 × 4-inch piece of red and green plaid fabric**

- **Ruler**

- **Scissors**

- **Needle**

- **Thread**

- **White glue or low temperature glue gun and glue sticks**

- **One 1½-inch spring barrette**

(continued on next page)

1. Cut each ball in half with a craft knife. Cut four 2½-inch diameter circles from the fabric. Sew a running stitch around the edge of each circle; pull slightly to form a pouch. Insert a half-ball, round side down, into each pouch. Pull gathers tightly. Knot and cut off the remaining thread.

2. Cut four ½-inch diameter circles from the remaining fabric. Glue the circles to the back of each half-ball, covering the gathers.

3. Glue the half-balls to the top of the spring barrette.

EARRINGS

MATERIALS

Same materials as for barrette on page 17, except for:

- **One ⅞-inch ball of STYROFOAM brand plastic foam**

- **5 × 5-inch piece of red and green plaid fabric**

- **One pair of earring posts and backs or clip backs**

1. Repeat Step 1 as it was described for the barrette.

2. Repeat Step 2 as it was described for the barrette. Glue on the earring backs.

Courtesy of The Dow Chemical Company. Designed by Maria Filosa, SCD.

❦ HOLIDAY SPIRIT ❦
SWEATSHIRT AND LEGGINGS

Use lovely Christmas paper napkins as an appliqué on
fabric? It's possible with Naplique Paper Adhesive.
Here's a new way to create beautiful design work on
fabric quickly, inexpensively, easily, and with washable
results!

MATERIALS

- **White sweatshirt**

- **White leggings**

- **Shirt board**

- **Masking tape**

- **Paper napkins of your choice**

- **Scissors**

- **Disappearing ink fabric marker**

- **Delta Transfer Naplique Paper Applique**

- **½-inch wide flat paintbrush**

- **Waxed paper**

- **Small water container for rinsing brushes**

- **Ruler**

- **Delta Starlite Fabric Dye in kelly green**

- **Delta Glitter Stuff for fabric in gold**

- **Small piece of cardboard**

*Note: Napkins are thin enough to glue to the fabric and strong enough for easy handling. Smaller designs work better than a large design. If you are working with a large design, try cutting it apart and reassembling it on the fabric surface.

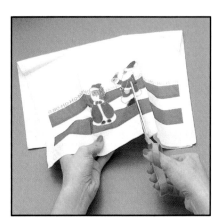

1. Prepare your shirt and leggings by washing and drying them as outlined on page 9. Tape the sweatshirt to the shirt board. Cut out your design through all plies (layers) of the napkin. (You can cut directly on the outline of the design or cut a general outline if it is too intricate.)

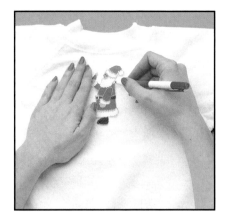

2. Plan how you will arrange your design by laying the napkin on the garment or fabric. (Patterns may be reversed.) With the design in place, trace around the cut edge of the napkin with the disappearing ink fabric marker. (Do not worry if disappearing ink marks the napkin.)

3. Use the paintbrush to apply a generous amount of Naplique inside and right up to the marker outline, directly on the fabric. Make sure you cover the entire area.

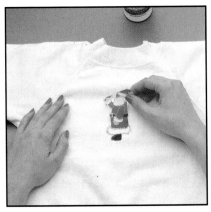

4. Lay the top ply of the cut napkin right-side up over the glue and quickly use a dry paintbrush to press it from the center to the outside edge. Lay a piece of waxed paper over the napkin appliqué at this point. Close the lid on your bottle of Naplique. Use the bottle as a rolling pin to roll out any air bubbles or wrinkles. Remove the waxed paper.

5. Cover and top-coat the entire design with Naplique. You do not have to wait until the Naplique you applied in step 4 is dry. Be sure to put Naplique over the cut edge of the napkin to seal it in. (Naplique is cloudy when applied but will dry clear.) Rinse your paintbrush.

6. Use a disappearing ink fabric marker and a ruler to measure and mark a $\frac{1}{2}$-inch wide stripe along the lower edge of your napkin design. Fill inside the disappearing lines with kelly green Fabric Dye.

Courtesy of Delta/Shiva Technical Coatings, Inc. Designed by Peggy Caldwell.

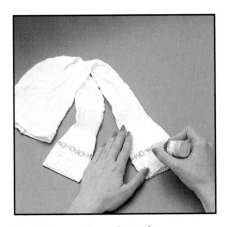

7. Write HO-HO-HO underneath the stripe and around the neck of the shirt with the gold Glitter Stuff.

8. Add cardboard to the bottoms of leggings to stretch the fabric. Write HO-HO-HO along the lace edge of the leggings with the gold Glitter Stuff. Accent your napkin design anywhere you think it would look nice.

ELEGANT POINSETTIA CARDIGAN

No one will ever know that this elegant holiday cardigan was a sweatshirt. Using fabric paint and some household staples, you can quickly create the beginnings of a wonderful holiday outfit. Wear this over slacks and a blouse and the Christmas tree will not be the only thing that shines in your house.

1. Prewash your sweatshirt following the instructions on page 9. Cover the work area with brown paper. Photocopy the pattern from page 24. Tape the tulle netting on top of the paper and on the work surface to secure. Trace the poinsettia pattern with the fine point permanent marker.

2. Attach the prewashed sweatshirt to the shirt board as described on page 8. Use a white pencil to draw a straight line down the center of the shirt. Transfer the poinsettia patterns through the tulle to the shirt using the white pencil. Be sure to watch the placement of the poinsettia flowers, keeping them at least 1 inch away from the center line.

MATERIALS

- Black sweatshirt— one size larger than you wear

- Brown paper or newspaper to cover the work area

- 9 × 15-inch piece of tulle netting

- Masking tape

- Fine point permanent marker

- Shirt board

- White pencil or tailor's chalk

- ½-inch wide flat paintbrush

- Tulip COVERS ALL paints in white, red, and dark green

- Small water container for rinsing brushes

- Waxed paper

- Standard household sponge cut in the shape of a holly leaf

- Tulip SOFT METALLICS paint in platinum

- Tulip Glitter dimensional fabric paint in champagne

- Tulip Pearl dimensional fabric paint in ruby red pearl

- Tulip Slick dimensional fabric paint in green

- Ruler

- Pinking shears

- Washable fabric glue

- Iron

3. Using the edge of a dry paintbrush, brush some COVERS ALL red paint along the top edge of the petals. Immediately begin to pull some of the paint into the center of the petal using the flat side of the paintbrush. Do not fill in the entire petal with paint. The black shirt will show through the thinner areas of paint.

(continued on next page)

4. Add additional paint in some areas to create highlights. Run a thin line of paint along the lower edge of the petal to define the bottom shape. Repeat for the other petals. Make some poinsettias red and others white. Be sure to thoroughly rinse out the paintbrush when changing paint colors.

5. Pour a small amount of the dark green COVERS ALL paint on a piece of waxed paper. Cover one side of the dry holly leaf-shaped sponge lightly with paint. Lightly sponge holly leaves between the poinsettias. Add additional paint to the waxed paper as needed.

6. Using the white pencil, draw in a ribbon. Fill in the area with the platinum SOFT METALLICS.

9. Let the sweatshirt dry flat overnight. Using pinking shears, cut down the center line of the sweatshirt front. Fold under approximately ½ inch on each side and iron the edge on the back side. Run a line of washable fabric glue under the edge and push down on the material to adhere. Let dry thoroughly. Heat-set COVERS ALL paint with a dry iron set to a temperature to match the fabric content of the sweatshirt.

Courtesy of Tulip/Polymerics, Inc. Designed by Lee Riggins-Hartman, SCD.

7. If desired, squeeze on a few thin accent lines to several poinsettia petals using the champagne Glitter fabric paint. Immediately brush out the paint into the petal. This will add a shimmer to a few petals (we only did this on the white poinsettias). Add "seeds" of champagne glitter to the center of each poinsettia.

8. Add a few beads of ruby red Pearl paint for holly berries between the leaves and flowers. Outline and vein each holly leaf using the green Slick paint. Do not make a solid line. Add a few tendrils between the leaves and flowers, if desired.

SNOWFLAKE SPLENDOR APRON AND MITTS

Are you in need of a simple, quick, relatively inexpensive gift to present to the hostess of a holiday party? This adorable apron is fast to make and looks great. It's also extremely practical—with all of the time spent in the kitchen during the holiday season, an apron is a very useful gift. If you're really ambitious, make an oven mitt and potholder to match.

MATERIALS

- **Red apron**

- **Brown paper or newspaper**

- **9 × 12-inch piece of fine tulle netting**

- **Fine point permanent marker**

- **Disappearing ink fabric marker**

- **One 1.25 oz. EASYFLOW bottle of Tulip CRYSTAL paint in icicle**

- **Twelve 10 or 12mm acrylic flat-backed crystal-clear rhinestones**

- **One 1.25 oz. EASYFLOW bottle of Tulip Glitter paint in gold**

- **Waxed paper**

- **Stiff bristle toothbrush**

- **Small piece of cardboard**

- **OPTIONAL: matching potholder and coordinated oven mitt**

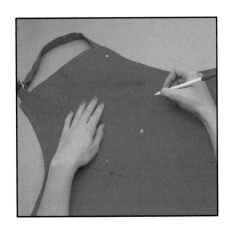

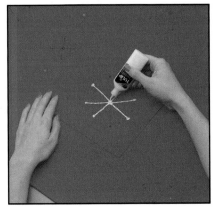

1. Prewash the apron using the directions on page 9. Cover your work area with brown paper or newspaper. Transfer the snowflake patterns on page 28 to the apron using the technique described in Step 1 on page 23. When you transfer the pattern, go over your lines again with disappearing ink fabric marker to make them clear.

2. Using the Tulip CRYSTAL icicle paint, squeeze on lines of paint following the transferred pattern. Lightly drag the tip of the bottle along the fabric surface for best paint adhesion. Do one snowflake at a time. Note that the paint will appear milky when first squeezed out of the bottle. As the paint dries, the base will turn clear and the glitter will show.

3. Complete one pattern at a time, adding rhinestone accents on each pattern as follows: Squeeze out a bead of the CRYSTAL icicle paint about the same size, shape, and thickness of the rhinestones you have selected. Carefully place the flat mirror-backed side of the stone into the bead of paint. Gently tap the center of the stone, setting it into the bead of paint. Paint must be totally under and around the edge of the stone in order to adhere. *(continued on next page)*

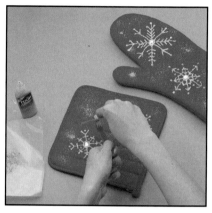

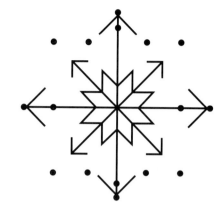

4. Squeeze a small amount of the gold Glitter paint on a piece of waxed paper. Dip a toothbrush into the paint. Holding the toothbrush in one hand, flick the bristles with a piece of cardboard to spatter. Repeat all over for a splattered look. Allow to dry overnight.

5. Repeat for oven mitt and potholder, if desired.

Courtesy of Tulip/Polymerics, Inc. Designed by Lee Riggins-Hartman, SCD.

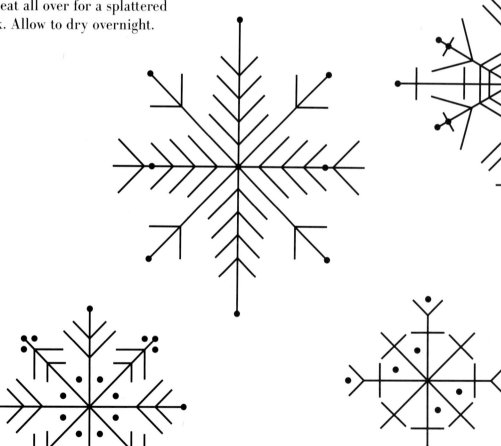

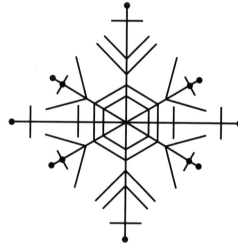

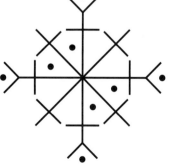

FROSTY SNOWMAN CENTERPIECE

Did you ever think how nice it would look if your Christmas dinner centerpiece looked as if it were made out of snow? This cheery fellow will certainly fool your guests as they wonder if he'll melt. Only you need to know how easy he is to make.

MATERIALS

- **Three foam balls—** 5-inch, 4-inch, 3-inch

- **Black & Decker low temperature glue gun and glue sticks**

- **One 3½-inch foam egg**

- **Serrated knife**

- **White, pink, red, and black acrylic paint**

- **¼-inch and ½-inch flat paintbrushes**

- **Small water container for rinsing brushes**

- **Felt—7 × 8 inches, black; 4 × 4 inches, red; 2 × 2 inches, orange**

- **Medium amount of fiberfill**

- **Wired silver ribbon—10 inches of ¹⁄₁₆-inch wide; 5 inches of ¼-inch wide, 2 inches of 2¾-inch wide**

- **Ruler**

- **Pompons—two 1-inch, red; three ½-inch, black**

- **Compass**

- **Scissors**

- **8½ inches of ¾-inch wide red satin ribbon**

- **White feather**

- **18 inches of ⅝-inch wide red nylon webbing**

- **Blunt-tipped needle**

- **3 inches of each—white and black baby rickrack**

- **8 × 8-inch square of silver metallic foil board**

- **Snow paint**

- **8-inch long 3mm dowel**

1. Body—Flatten the top and bottom of the 5-inch and 4-inch foam balls by placing them on a table and pressing down to flatten a 2-inch diameter circle. Flatten the bottom of the 3-inch foam ball.

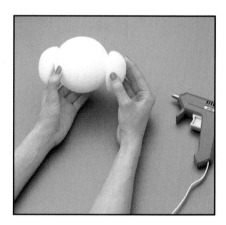

2. Arms—Cut the foam egg in half lengthwise using a serrated knife. Glue the cut side of an egg half to a side of the 4-inch foam ball with the narrow end of the egg slightly forward. Repeat for the other arm. With the ½-inch paintbrush, paint this section white and let it dry. Rinse the brush.

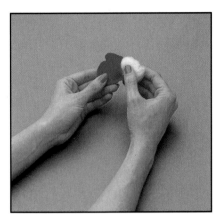

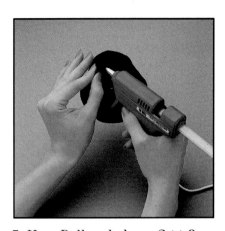

3. Mittens—Cut two mittens from the red felt according to the pattern. Keeping the sides aligned, pull back half of the top layer and apply a line of glue ¼ inch from the edge. Press the felt into place. Glue the other edges, leaving the straight edge unglued. Stuff the mitten lightly with fiberfill. Glue straight edges around the narrow end of the arm. Repeat for the other mitten.

4. Earmuffs—Paint the 3-inch ball white and let it dry. Rinse the brush. Shape a 5-inch length of ¼-inch wide wired silver ribbon into a curve. Glue it over the top of the head. Trim one side of red pompon and glue the flat side to the side of the head, covering the end of the wired ribbon. Repeat for the other side.

5. Hat—Roll and glue a 2 × 8-inch piece of black felt into a cylinder with 2-inch edges slightly overlapping. Determine the diameter of the cylinder and use a compass to draw the same size black felt circle. (Approximate size will be 2½ inches.) Cut out the circle and glue it to the top of the cylinder. For the brim, cut a 4-inch black felt circle and cut out a 2¼-inch circle in the center. Glue the bottom of the cylinder to the brim, covering the circular opening. Wrap a 8½-inch length of red satin ribbon around the crown, overlapping and gluing the ends in back. Glue the end of the feather behind the ribbon on the side of the hat. Lightly stuff the hat with fiberfill. Glue the hat to the snowman's head.

(continued on next page)

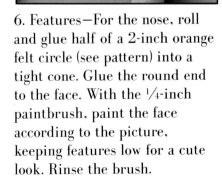

6. Features—For the nose, roll and glue half of a 2-inch orange felt circle (see pattern) into a tight cone. Glue the round end to the face. With the ¼-inch paintbrush, paint the face according to the picture, keeping features low for a cute look. Rinse the brush.

mitten

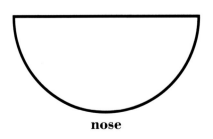

nose

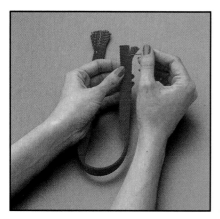

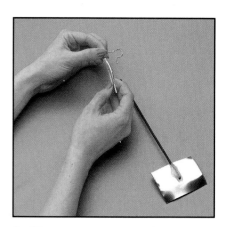

7. Scarf—Use scissors to trim off 1 inch of "braided thread" from the end of an 18-inch length of nylon webbing. Use a needle to pull apart the threads to "frizz." Glue a 1½-inch length of white rickrack ½ inch from the frizzed end, wrapping and gluing the ends around the sides to the back. Repeat with a 1½-inch length of black rickrack, positioning it ½ inch above the white rickrack. Repeat for the other end of the scarf. Wrap the scarf around the neck. Tie half a square knot in front and glue to hold.

8. Snow—Cut an 8-inch circle of silver metallic foil board and trim the edges into gentle curves. Paint the board, using the ½-inch paintbrush with snow paint. Rinse the brush. Let dry. Paint the 5-inch ball white and let it dry. Glue it to the bottom of the glued and painted balls to form the snowman. Glue the bottom of the snowman to the center of the painted board.

9. Shovel—With the ½-inch paintbrush, paint an 8-inch dowel black. Rinse the brush. Let dry. Glue a 2-inch length of 2¾-inch wide wired silver ribbon to the end of the dowel. For the handle, twist together two 5-inch lengths of 1¹⁄₁₆-inch wide wired silver ribbon. Wrap one end around the end of the dowel and extend it ¼ inch. Bend the twisted ribbon up ¼ inch, over ¾ inch, down ¼ inch, and back over to the dowel. Position the handle in the right mitten and glue it to the mitten and snowman.

10. Buttons—Trim one side of three black pompons and glue the flat sides to the front of the snowman according to the finished photo.

Courtesy of Black & Decker.
Designed by Cindy Groom Harry and staff.

CHRISTMAS TREE SERVING TRAY

Serving trays are certainly a practical idea for
Christmas—especially ones that are this easy and fast to
paint. This country-look pattern is adorned with lovely
Christmas trees. Not a bit of holiday spirit is lost.

MATERIALS

- **Brown paper or newspaper**

- **Piece of cardboard**

- **Pencil**

- **Scissors**

- **Unfinished tray of choice**

- **One bottle of Delta Home Decor stain resist**

- **Scrap paper**

- **Color wipes or soft rag**

- **One bottle of each— Delta Home Decor pickling gel: navy blue, forest green**

- **One bottle of Delta gold base coat**

- **Household sponge**

- **Stiff bristle toothbrush**

- **One bottle of Delta Hallmark Home Decor acrylic water-based varnish**

- **½-inch wide flat paintbrush**

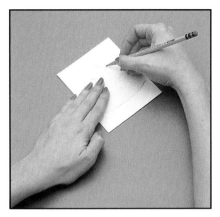

1. Cover the work area with brown paper or newspaper. Photocopy the tree pattern and trace it on a piece of cardboard. Cut it out.

2. Place the cardboard pattern inside the tray. Trace lightly around the edge with a pencil, creating the pattern of your choice.

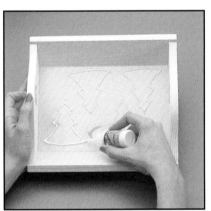

3. Practice a few lines with stain resist on a piece of paper before beginning the tree design to get the feel of how it flows from the bottle. Draw a line with the stain resist just inside the pencil line. Do not draw directly over pencil lines. The stain resist line is cloudy as it is applied but will dry clear. When the resist is completely clear, it is dry enough for the next step.

4. Use a color wipe or a soft rag to wipe the stain on the tray. Alternate colors of navy blue and forest green. Make sure that you softly blend one color into another where they touch. Dampen one end of your cloth and wipe away the centers of your trees. Color will not adhere to the wood resist lines. If you want the stain to be darker, let it dry for about 30 minutes and reapply.

5. Trace the star on a piece of cardboard. Cut it out to form a stencil.

6. Lay the stencil at the top of the tree. Use the sponge to stipple metallic gold base coat through the star stencil opening. Alternate sides and trees and repeat stippling.

7. Load your toothbrush with metallic gold paint. Hold the brush approximately 6 inches from the tray. Use a small piece of cardboard to pull and scrape across the bristles of your toothbrush, spattering the tray with gold flecks.

8. When the spatter is completely dry, varnish the tray with several coats of matte varnish using a ¹/₂-inch flat paintbrush.

Courtesy of Delta/Shiva Technical Coatings, Inc. Designed by Peggy Caldwell.

PICTURE PERFECT KRINKLES FRAME

Framed photographs are popular Christmas gifts for a
good reason. They not only showcase a loved one's
picture, they do so in a festive fashion. Can you think
of a more appropriate frame than one that you
decorated yourself for a completely personalized gift?

1. Using a low temperature glue gun, apply a line of glue to the inside top edge of the picture frame and glue the ruffle in place. Begin and end 1 inch below the upper left-hand corner, placing the flat edge of the ruffle closest to the glass.

2. Cut a 48-inch piece from each KRINKLES color. Place a dot of low temperature glue on the ends and glue them together.

3. Glue joined ends to the upper left-hand corner of the frame directly above the gathered edge of fabric. Begin twisting both colors of KRINKLES together. Glue twisted KRINKLES around the picture frame directly over the gathered edge. Cut off excess and glue the ends together. Glue these ends to the frame.

MATERIALS

- **One 5 × 7-inch picture frame and photo**

- **28 inches of 1½-inch pregathered Christmas ruffle or lace**

- **Low temperature glue gun and glue sticks**

- **Approximately 65 inches of red/gold center #92G KRINKLES**

- **Approximately 65 inches of green satin/gold edge #97G KRINKLES**

- **Scissors**

4. Cut remaining lengths of KRINKLES into two 5-inch pieces and two 10-inch pieces. Using the 5-inch pieces, place green and red KRINKLES in an "X" over the upper left-hand corner of the picture frame. Glue in place.

5. Using the remaining 10-inch pieces, tie a simple bow with each color. Glue each bow separately to the upper left-hand corner of the frame directly on top of the center of the "X."

Courtesy of Karen's Kreations.
Designed by Kim and Judy Kley.

JOY—OLD WORLD SERVING TRAY

This cross-stitch serving tray will become a treasured heirloom. Classic nesting dolls stitched in rich colors lend this project an antique look, while the glass covering makes it easy to keep clean. This is truly a piece that all of your guests will comment on!

MATERIALS

- **One 11 × 8 inch piece of 14-count Aida cloth**

- **6-strand cotton embroidery floss (see color key)**

- **Embroidery hoop (optional)**

- **Scissors**

- **#24 tapestry needle**

- **Sudberry House Serving Tray in dark brown #65651 or any frame of choice**

- **Phillips head screwdriver (only necessary if you are using the Sudberry tray)**

- **Masking tape**

Following the general instructions on page 5, stitch according to the chart. When completed, follow the instructions supplied with the tray to mount the project.

Courtesy of The DMC Corporation. Designed by Ursula Michael.

Stitch count: 99w × 65h
Size: #14—7 × 5¹/₂ inches

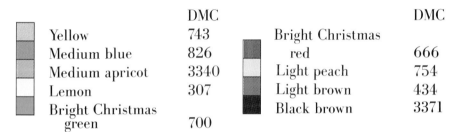

		DMC			DMC
	Yellow	743		Bright Christmas red	666
	Medium blue	826		Light peach	754
	Medium apricot	3340		Light brown	434
	Lemon	307		Black brown	3371
	Bright Christmas green	700			

YULETIDE WREATH

Wreaths are always popular at Christmastime. This red and green version made of natural materials is certainly destined to be a classic. The preserved greenery and eucalyptus add just the right color and texture.

1. Glue the dry foam to the bottom of the wreath using the hot glue gun. Fasten it with wire. Cover the foam lightly with Spanish moss and secure it with greening pins.

2. Insert the red cedar roses vertically, one below the next. Also add the preserved eucalyptus vertically.

3. Layer three mushrooms in a terracing fashion from bottom to top, starting from largest to smallest. Insert the remaining mushroom at a 45-degree angle at the right of the block of foam.

MATERIALS

- **18-inch red rope and vine wreath (or any other 18-inch wreath)**

- **3 × 3-inch block of dry foam**

- **Hot glue gun and glue sticks**

- **Floral wire**

- **Handful of Spanish moss**

- **Greening pins**

- **Six dried red cedar roses (or other dried pod flowers sprayed red)**

- **Six stems of preserved eucalyptus**

- **Four dried sponge mushrooms**

- **Two stems of preserved juniper**

- **Four stems of preserved cedar**

- **Wood picks**

- **Florist tape**

- **Half a bunch of dried red star flowers**

- **Half a bunch of dried red edelweiss (or red button flowers)**

4. Insert the juniper and cedar in an S-shaped curve from top left to bottom right. Use wood picks to reinforce stems, if necessary. Tape clusters of the red star flowers and red edelweiss to wood picks. Insert them in the arrangement, following the curves and lines of the greenery.

Designed by Maria Buscemi.

SEASON'S SWEETEST CANDY DISH

Candy is a Christmas tradition. And when you want to create a lovely, quick, and easy plastic canvas candy dish you can do so in no time. This incredibly versatile container looks pretty as a plant holder, too.

Read the information on plastic canvas on page 6. Cut out and stitch the pattern on all eight side pieces. The star in the center of each side piece is made with the Smyrna stitch. Stitch the star according to the diagram: The needle comes up through the odd-numbered holes and goes down through the even-numbered holes.

MATERIALS

• **One sheet of white 7-count Darice plastic canvas**

• **Scissors**

• **#18 tapestry needle**

• **Darice nylon plus plastic canvas yarn (see color key)**

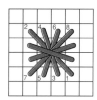

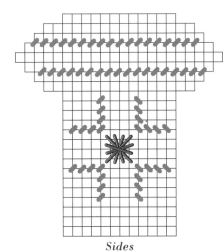

Sides

Overcast-stitch the sides of all eight pieces together, forming a circle. Overcast-stitch the circle of side pieces to the bottom. On the angled parts of the bottom, you'll have to fit in stitches to attach the sections. Overcast-stitch around the top of the basket.

Courtesy of Nifty Publishing Company. Designed by Lynda Scott Musante, SCD.

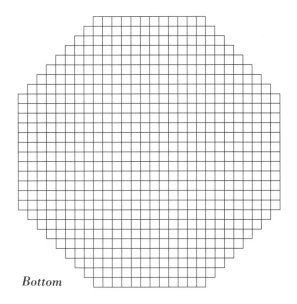

Bottom

		Darice
▨	Holly green	31 (8 yards)
▨	Christmas red	19 (18 yards)

BEJEWELED NOTECARD

This bright and shiny notecard will add that special touch to your Christmas greetings. Just punch a hole through the top and send your loved ones an ornament.

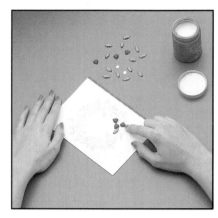

1. Photocopy the pattern from the book. Trim around the pattern so that there is not much excess. Place a square of carbon paper underneath the pattern and lightly tape both layers to the front of the card. Firmly trace the pattern with a ballpoint pen. Remove the carbon paper and the pattern.

2. Using white glue, lightly coat the back (or foil side) of each of the stones. Press the stones gently into place foil-side down according to the shape outline and color code. Repeat with all stones, one at a time, until all shape outlines are covered. Draw in the leaves with the green marker.

- **One 7 × 5-inch blank card and matching envelope**

- **Carbon paper**

- **Ballpoint pen**

- **Sixteen 10 × 9mm Foil-back Acrylic Faceted Hearts—Ruby**

- **Four 7mm Foil-back round Faceted Acrylic Stones—Crystal**

- **Sixteen 15 × 7mm Foil-back Navettes— Emerald**

- **White glue or low temperature glue gun and glue sticks**

- **Green marker**

Courtesy of The Beadery Craft Products.

BENDABLE RIBBON ADORNMENTS

These bendable ribbon ornaments are fun for kids of all ages. You can use them to decorate your packages or to adorn your tree. They are so simple to make that you will soon be coming up with your own designs. Just use your imagination!

MATERIALS

- **Pencil**

- **Masking tape**

- **Bedford Bendable Ribbon—18 inches of ¼-inch wide Majestic Red; 18 inches of ¼-inch wide Majestic Silver; 9 inches of ¼-inch wide Majestic Green; and 6 inches of ¹⁄₁₆-inch wide Majestic Green**

- **Wire cutters**

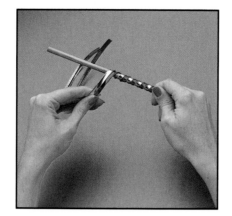

1. Use masking tape to secure one end of an 18-inch length of ¼-inch wide Majestic Red and an 18-inch length of ¼-inch wide Majestic Silver bendable ribbon to one end of a pencil, positioned diagonally, side by side. Overhand-wrap both lengths of the bendable ribbon around the length of the pencil, keeping lengths parallel with each other while wrapping. As you reach the end of the pencil, remove the tape and slide the bendable ribbon spiral up, giving more pencil length to complete the spiral wrapping.

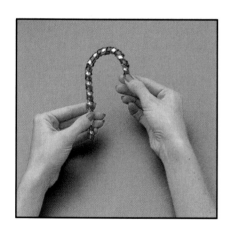

2. Remove the spiraled lengths of bendable ribbon from the pencil. Gently bend over approximately 2½ inches at one end of the spiral to form a candy cane.

3. Fold a 9-inch length of ¼-inch wide Majestic Green bendable ribbon to form a bow. Wrap a 6-inch length of ¹⁄₁₆-inch wide Majestic Green bendable ribbon around the center of the folded bow, twisting together the ends on the back to secure. (Note: Do not trim ends of center wrap.)

4. Insert one extended end of the bow binding through one spiral of the candy cane, about 3 inches up from bottom. Twist with the other end of the bow binding until it is securely attached to the candy cane. Trim ends. Angle the cut ends of the bow.

Courtesy of Bedford Industries, Inc. Designed by Cindy Groom Harry and staff.

❧ SPIRAL WREATH ❧

1. Repeat step 1 from the candy cane project, using a 24-inch length of ³⁄₄-inch wide Majestic Green bendable ribbon. After you remove the spiraled length of bendable ribbon from the pencil, grasp each end of the spiral. Twist one end gently clockwise, while twisting the other end gently counter-clockwise, forming a slightly larger diameter spiral than the diameter of the pencil.

2. Snip halfway through the bendable ribbon ¹⁄₄ inch from one end. Repeat on the other end. Bring the ends of the spiral together to form a circle, interlocking the notched ends.

3. Notch the ends of an 8-inch length of ¹⁄₄-inch wide Majestic Red bendable ribbon as you did for the wreath. Bring the ends together to form a circle and interlock the notched ends. Position the circle on edge with interlocking ends at the top of the circle. Gently push the interlocking ends down to the bottom of the circle, forming two loops on either side of the center. Position the middle of an 8-inch length of ¹⁄₄-inch wide Majestic Red bendable ribbon lengthwise on the top center of the loops. Wrap another 8-inch length of ¹⁄₄-inch wide Majestic Red bendable ribbon around the center of the bow and tail pieces, tightly twisting the ends together on the back.

4. Bend the tails down and fan them apart. Spiral-wrap each tail around the end of a pencil. Insert the end of a 6-inch length of the ¹⁄₁₆-inch wide Majestic Red bendable ribbon through the twist at the back of the bow. Position the bow on top of the interlocked ends on the wreath. Wrap the ends of the ¹⁄₁₆-inch wide length around the wreath to the inside of the spiral and tightly twist ends together to secure the bow on the wreath.

MATERIALS

- **Pencil**

- **Masking tape**

- **Bedford Bendable Ribbon—24 inches of ³⁄₄-inch wide Majestic Green; 24 inches of ¹⁄₄-inch Majestic Red; and 6 inches of ¹⁄₁₆-inch wide Majestic Red**

- **Wire cutters**

Courtesy of Bedford Industries, Inc. Designed by Cindy Groom Harry and staff.

YESTERYEAR TRIMMINGS

Personalized ornaments make wonderful tree
trimmings. If you insert a photo or cross-stitched
holiday greeting for decoration, you can have a really
unique Christmas memento. These unusual quick-tuck
ornaments are easy and quick to make.

CROSS-STITCH VARIATION

MATERIALS

- **6 × 18 × ½-inch piece of STYROFOAM brand plastic foam, cut into three 6 × 6-inch squares**

- **Ruler**

- **Ballpoint pen**

- **¼ yard each of cotton fabric—green solid, red micro print, and white, red, and green print**

- **Scissors**

- **Paring knife**

- **3 × 3-inch square of 4-count Aida cloth**

- **#24 tapestry needle**

- **Red embroidery floss**

- **1½ × 2-inch photo of choice**

- **White glue or low temperature glue gun and glue sticks**

- **4 yards of ¼-inch wide ribbon: red or green**

- **Six straight pins**

1. Photocopy the pattern from the book. Transfer it to a square of STYROFOAM brand plastic foam by pressing hard enough on a ballpoint pen to score. Retrace the pattern on the STYROFOAM brand plastic foam with the pen.

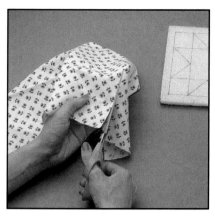

2. Cut fabric as follows: four 1¾-inch squares for "D" from white, green, and red print; two 2¼-inch squares for "B" from green fabric—cut each in half to create four triangles; four 3 × 1¾-inch rectangles for "C" from red micro print; and one 7 × 7-inch square from red micro print for backing.

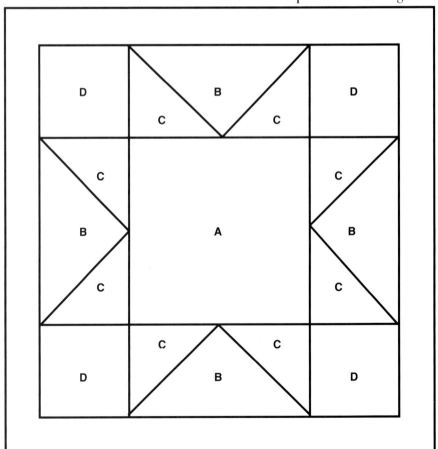

3. Center one corner square "D" over its block on the STYROFOAM brand plastic foam. With the tip of the knife, feel the score line of the pattern. Holding the knife vertically, push the fabric into the STYROFOAM brand plastic foam along the score line. The crisp texture of the STYROFOAM brand plastic foam will hold the fabric in place. This technique is called quick-tuck. Trim any excess fabric and tuck in any stray fabric edges. Repeat with remaining corners and large triangle pieces "B."

4. Center a 3 × 1¾-inch piece over a pair of small triangles "C." Quick-tuck along the center square and corner squares. Slit the center of the fabric at the top of triangle "B." Quick-tuck along the sides of triangle "B." Clip excess fabric. Repeat for other "C" triangles.

5. Cut center block "A" from the cross-stitch fabric. Backstitch the greeting. Do a trial fitting of the square over the STYROFOAM brand plastic foam. Cut fabric so that it just barely tucks in. Apply a small amount of glue along the back side of edges to prevent the Aida cloth from fraying. Quick-tuck in place, making sure glued edges stick to the STYROFOAM brand plastic foam.

■	DMC
Bright Christmas red	666

6. Center the STYROFOAM brand plastic foam on the wrong side of backing fabric. Wrap all four edges to the front and quick-tuck along the border line. Miter corners neatly. Quick-tuck corners along the diagonal.

7. Tie two small ribbon bows and cut one 12-inch long ribbon hanger. Attach bows and the hanger to the top of the ornament by pushing straight pins through the ribbon and into the STYROFOAM brand plastic foam.

🌿 PHOTO VARIATION 🌿

1. Repeat Step 1 from page 50.

2. Cut fabric as follows: four 1³⁄₄-inch squares for "D" from white, green, and red print; two 2¹⁄₄-inch squares for "B" from green fabric—cut each in half to create four triangles; four 3 × 1³⁄₄-inch rectangles for "C" from red micro print; and one 7 × 7-inch square from green solid for backing.

3. Repeat Step 3 from page 51.

4. Repeat Step 4 from page 51. Cut center block "A." On the back of the fabric, draw an opening for the picture in the center. Cut the opening diagonally from the upper left to lower right corners, and from upper right to lower left

corners. Fold the fabric to the back side along the drawn line and lightly glue in place. Glue the photo to the STYROFOAM brand plastic foam in the center of block "A." Quick-tuck prepared fabric block "A" over the photograph.

5. Repeat Step 6 from page 51.

6. Repeat Step 7 from page 51.

🌿 ALL-FABRIC VARIATION 🌿

1. Repeat Step 1 from page 50.

2. Cut fabric as follows: four 1³⁄₄-inch squares for "D" from white, green, and red print; two 2¹⁄₄-inch squares for "B" from white, green, and red print—cut each in half to create four triangles; one 5¹⁄₂-inch square for center panel from red micro print; and one 7 × 7-inch square from green solid for backing.

3. Repeat Step 3 from page 51. Center the 5¹⁄₂-inch square of fabric over center block "A." Remove a 1¹⁄₄-inch square from each corner. Center the fabric over the STYROFOAM brand plastic foam. Quick-tuck along the inside edges of the cut-out corners. Slit the fabric to the center point over the large

triangle. Quick-tuck along the triangle.

4. Repeat Step 6 from page 51.

5. Repeat Step 7 from page 51.

Courtesy of The Dow Chemical Company. Designed by Susan Laity Price, SCD.

HANGING CAROUSEL CRITTERS

You can almost hear the merry-go-round music as these
carousel animals sparkle on the tree. The beautiful
colors make these ornaments lovely Christmas
keepsakes to use year after year. And they're
surprisingly easy to make.

MATERIALS

• **Four sheets of 14-count clear Darice plastic canvas**

• **#22 tapestry needle**

• **Scissors**

• **Kreinik Metallic #16 braid (see color key)**

Read the plastic canvas information on page 6. Using the continental stitch, stitch each side of the design on 14-count plastic canvas with one strand of #16 braid according to the pattern. Be sure to position the design on the canvas sheet with enough room all around it to cut it out. Bold lines indicate individual stitches. Stitch two of each pattern as shown, making sure to reverse one so that you have a left and a right side.

When completed, very carefully cut out the designs, leaving one bar of plastic canvas all around the design. Match the pieces on their wrong sides and begin overcasting edges together, matching colors. Cut an 8- to 9-inch piece of metallic floss (color of your choice). Insert one end through the knob at the top of the pole and pull the ends to match. Tie the ends in a knot about ½ inch down from the ends to form a hanger.

Courtesy of Kreinik Manufacturing, Inc. Designed by Carole Rodgers, SCD.

RABBIT	Kreinik
Pink	007
Black	005HL
Gold	002
Amethyst	026
Red	003
Green	008
Silver	001
Pearl	032

ROOSTER	
Gold	002
Silver	001
Chartreuse	015
Turquoise	029
Citron	028
Black	005HL
Red	003
Colonial red	308

CAMEL	
Gold	002
Red	003
Sapphire	051HL
Chartreuse	015
Silver	001
Black	005HL
Brown	022
Copper	021

FROG	
Gold	002
Black	005HL
Red	003
Silver	001
Sapphire	051HL
Green	008
Chartreuse	015

(continued on next page)

BRIGHT AND
SHINY ORNAMENTS

Fabric-embellished ornaments are always beautiful, but
expensive. Now you can create your own variations
with simple shiny ornaments, a bit of ribbon, and a lot
of imagination. Your guests will find it hard to believe
that you made these ornaments yourself.

❧ SHINY GOLD ❧

MATERIALS

- **10 inches of red satin/gold edge #96G KRINKLES**
- **10 inches of green satin/gold edge #97G KRINKLES**
- **Scissors**
- **One 3-inch shiny gold ornament**
- **Low temperature glue gun and glue sticks**
- **8 inches of ⅛-inch wide green satin ribbon**

1. Make four small KRINKLES balls in each color. To make balls use uncut length of KRINKLES and tie a single knot. Tighten the knot to form a pleasing appearance. Cut off the remaining KRINKLES ½ inch from either side of the knot. Turn the ends to the back side of the knot and glue to the underside of the knot.

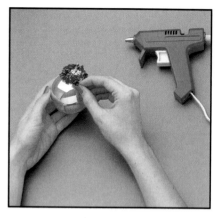

2. Using a low temperature glue gun, glue alternating colors of small KRINKLES balls around the edge of the metal hanger on the gold ornament. Cut the ⅛-inch wide green satin ribbon into an 8-inch length. Tie the lengths to the gold metal hanger with simple single knots.

❧ SHINY RED ❧

MATERIALS

- **One 3-inch shiny red ornament**
- **One triple-leaf holly sprig**
- **8 inches of red satin/gold edge #96G KRINKLES**
- **Scissors**
- **Low temperature glue gun and glue sticks**
- **9 inches of ¼-inch wide red satin ribbon**

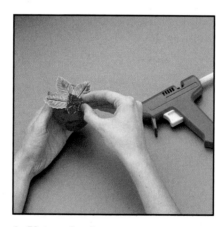

1. Using the low temperature glue gun, glue the holly sprig to the center front of the ornament. Make three small

KRINKLES balls from red satin/gold edge KRINKLES as described in Step 1 above. Glue KRINKLES balls on the top of the base of the holly sprig in a staggered arrangement. Tie the ¼-inch wide red satin ribbon to the ornament's metal hanger.

Courtesy of Karen's Kreations.
Designed by Kim and Judy Kley.

TWINKLE ANGEL
TREE TOPPER

This graceful angel looks as elegant and dainty as a
porcelain doll. It's a wonderful addition to any
beautifully decorated tree and will elicit lots of praise
from people wondering how in the world you made it.
Only you need to know how really easy it is!

MATERIALS

- **36 inches of untwisted white TISSUE TWIST**

- **Scissors**

- **White glue or low temperature glue gun and glue sticks**

- **24 gauge gold-tone craft wire**

- **1¼-inch porcelain doll head and matching doll hands**

- **36 inches of untwisted Twinkle, Twinkle TISSUE TWIST**

- **One white chenille stem**

- **6½-inch wing span gold angel wings**

- **Hot glue gun and glue sticks**

- **Wire cutters (optional)**

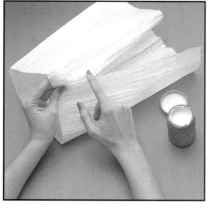

1. For the underskirt, cut three 12-inch lengths of white TISSUE TWIST. Glue them together with white glue, side by side with a ½-inch overlap along the 12-inch edges to form a tube.

2. Fold the open end of the tube over the outside until the two open ends are even. Gather the folded edge of the tube and secure it with craft wire approximately ½ inch from the folded edge. Insert and glue the gathered end of the tube into the bottom of the porcelain head.

3. Cut four 5½-inch lengths of Twinkle, Twinkle TISSUE TWIST. Glue them together side by side with a ½-inch overlap along the 5½-inch edges to form a tube. Cut a scallop edge on one open end of the tube. Slide the tube over the head and underskirt with the scallop edge at the bottom.

4. Gather around the neck with approximately ¾ inch extending above the neck to form a collar. Secure the gather around the neck with a 6-inch length of craft wire. Trim the excess wire. Pull the collar down and fluff.

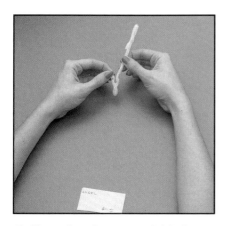

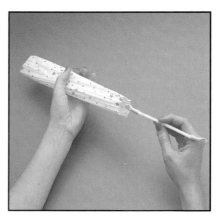

5. To make the arms, fold the ends back on a chenille stem and twist them so that they are 5 inches long. Glue one hand to each end of the stem.

6. Cut a 10-inch length of Twinkle, Twinkle TISSUE TWIST. Glue the 10-inch edges together with a $\frac{1}{2}$-inch overlap to form a tube. Slide the arms into the tube. Gather the tube around the wrist so that the end of the tube extends approximately $\frac{1}{4}$ inch onto the hand. Wire the gather to secure it. Repeat with the other wrist. Adjust the fullness of the sleeves by pulling excess toward the hands. Flare the cuffs. Gather slightly in the center of the arms and hot glue to the back, just below the collar.

7. Glue the wings to the back with the hot glue gun. If the angel is not to be hung on a tree, use wire cutters to clip the hook just above the halo.

Courtesy of MPR Associates, Inc. Designed by Fran Queen.

SPIRITED PLASTIC CANVAS EMBELLISHMENTS

These three wonderful Christmas ornaments are old standbys with lots of flair. The rocking horse, Santa, and a bright red cardinal are so easy to make and so much fun to have around. You'll be reminded of your own childhood when you proudly hung handmade ornaments.

Read the instructions on plastic canvas on page 6. Stitch the shapes according to the patterns. Be sure to position the designs on the canvas sheet so that there is enough room all around them to cut them out. When completed, very carefully cut out the designs leaving one bar of plastic canvas around each. Match the wrong sides of the pieces together. Overcast-stitch the edges with matching colors.

To make the cardinal, overcast-stitch the edges of the wings stopping at the top edge. Hold the wings against the body. The bold line on the patterns near the shoulder of each side indicates where the wing should be attached. Continue to overcast-stitch attaching the wing, bringing the needle down through the body section, too. Match the wrong sides of the pieces together and begin overcasting the edges together. Begin at the beak and work your way down the back and around the body. Be sure to match yarn colors as you go. Before closing up the stomach area, stuff the body with enough cotton balls to fill. Finish stitching. For a hanging loop, cut a 6-inch piece of nylon thread; thread it through the top hole and knot the ends together.

Courtesy of Nifty Publishing Company. Designed by Lynda Scott Musante, SCD.

MATERIALS

- **One sheet of 7-count clear Darice plastic canvas**

- **Scissors**

- **#18 tapestry needle**

- **Darice Nylon Plus plastic canvas yarn (see color key)**

- **Handful of cotton balls**

- **Nylon thread**

ROCKING HORSE Darice

▨	Maple brown	35 (20 yards)
▨	Royal blue	09 (5 yards)
☐	Yellow	26 (5 yards)
▨	Christmas red	19 (15 yards)
■	Black	02 (1 yard)

SANTA

☐	Baby pink	10 (5 yards)
■	Royal blue	09 (1 yard)
☐	White	01 (14 yards)
▨	Christmas red	19 (10 yards)

CARDINAL

▨	Christmas red	19 (18 yards)
▨	Cinnamon	20 (16 yards)
☐	Yellow	26 (1 yard)
■	Black	02 (1 yard)

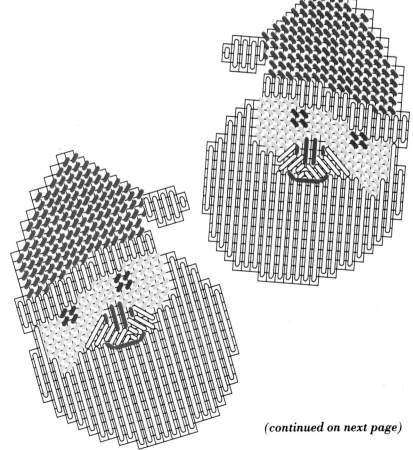

(continued on next page)

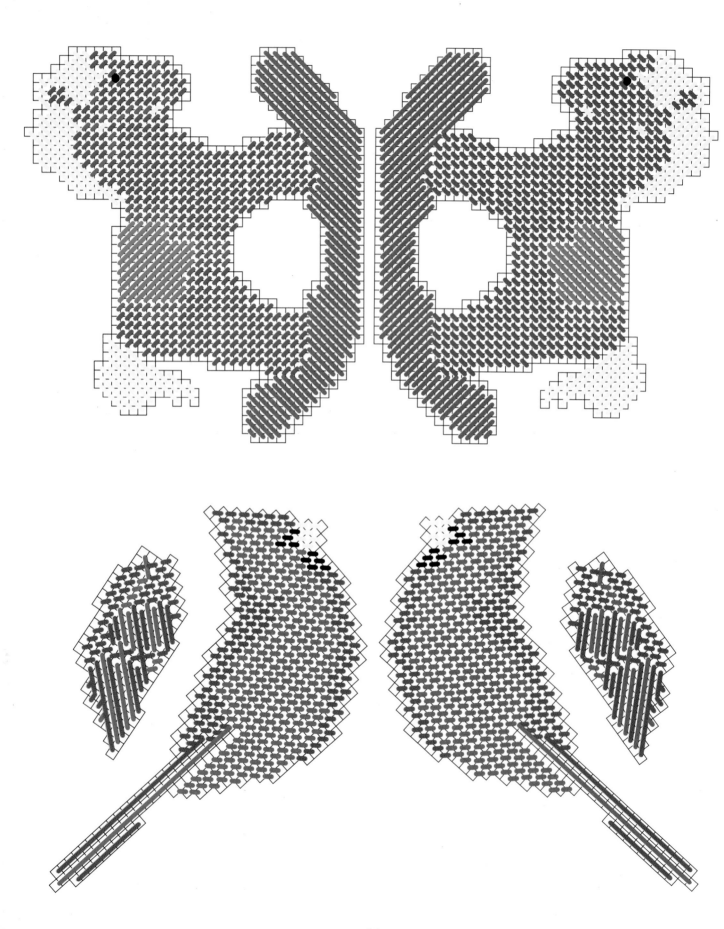